THE KINFOLK HOME

THE KINFOLK HOME

INTERIORS *for* SLOW LIVING

NATHAN WILLIAMS

Ouur

KRISTOFER JOHNSSON — Kristofer is a photographer living in Stockholm, Sweden, who shoots interiors and still-life images. His clean and simple aesthetic uses light and composition to focus on an image's natural beauty.

ANDERS SCHØNNEMANN — Anders is a lifestyle and interiors photographer based in Copenhagen, Denmark. Although he travels a lot for his work, he thinks there's nothing better than flying home to his wife and two daughters.

PIA ULIN — Pia is a Swedish photographer currently living in Brooklyn, New York. She primarily shoots interiors and lifestyle images but also dabbles in still-life photography that focuses on the intricate details.

SHARYN CAIRNS — Sharyn is a photographer from Melbourne, Australia. She enjoys shooting in a variety of styles and is inspired by the constant change and excitement that each new project brings.

JONAS INGERSTEDT — Jonas is an interiors photographer living in Stockholm, Sweden. After spending some time in Paris and 20 years as a fashion photographer, he's been shooting homes for the past four years.

SIMON WATSON — Simon is a portrait, interiors and travel photographer who splits his time between New York and Dublin, Ireland. He focuses on light and shadows and renders a holistic view of his subjects.

MIRJAM BLEEKER — Mirjam is a Dutch interiors and travel photographer living in Amsterdam, the Netherlands. She works with Frank Visser and feels grateful that her passion has allowed her to meet so many interesting people.

NICOLE FRANZEN — Nicole is a photographer based in Brooklyn, New York, who mostly shoots food and lifestyle images. Her elegant and clean aesthetic emphasizes natural light and finding beauty in the details.

MARTIN GUGGISBERG — Martin is both an interiors and architecture photographer and filmmaker based in Zurich, Switzerland. He is passionate about photojournalism and narrative-driven art.

DOMINIK TARABANSKI — Dominik is a Polish photographer living in New York. The cover of this book is a testament to his conceptual style that draws inspiration from the modern human form.

For a full list of credits, please see page 367.

CONTENTS

HOMES FOR SIMPLICITY

HOMES FOR SLOW LIVING

NATHAN WILLIAMS AND KATIE SEARLE–WILLIAMS
PORTLAND, OREGON, UNITED STATES

INTRODUCTION

The phrase "slow living" often brings to mind images of work-free days spent reclining in a hammock, piña colada in hand. While this may be the case at a beachside retreat in the Bahamas, the reality for most of us is that slow living takes many different forms in many different spaces. For some this could mean long Sunday mornings spent reading in bed with loved ones, and for others it could mean waking at dawn for the vim and vigor of a brisk swim. Slow living means something personal to each of us, and one of the strongest ways we manifest these beliefs is by expressing ourselves through our homes.

The slow approach to crafting a home is subjective to each dweller's aspirations, but it always finds its foundation in our deepest values. It's not about luxury or laziness, nor is it about forgoing our most beloved belongings: Slow living isn't about determining how little we can live with—it's about working out what we simply can't live without.

Our homes should explore life's fundamentals and then seek to incorporate them into our surroundings. In this way, a home isn't just a physical structure, but also a structure of our beliefs. A house should represent the heart, the kernel, the bedrock of our values—whatever brings us back to our cores. While "living essentially" can make us think of bare bookshelves or an empty wardrobe containing only white cotton T-shirts, we're able to invite slowness and simplicity into our days without prescribing to a predetermined aesthetic; this is because slow living is less of a style and more of a deeply personal mentality.

The function of our homes should dictate the way we decorate them, not the other way around. Instead of either clogging our lives with unnecessary clutter—both physical and mental—or needlessly throwing out meaningful possessions, we can work to determine what brings fulfillment to our lives, and then surround ourselves with those comforts.

A person's domestic space speaks of his or her innermost beliefs—consider what our belongings say about our character, be it a collection of inherited French antiques, a table long enough for a dinner party of a dozen, a smattering of children's sketches pasted on the walls or the absence of objects in a minimal space, leaving room for creative thought. The key to all these spaces' hearts is that their aesthetics are shaped by their dwellers' definitions of what brings joy and meaning to their homes. To us, this intention is the most important aspect of slow living.

While our homes can function as places we retreat to, we also seek to connect within them. In this way, they become active participants in our lives—living organisms that grow and shrink and change, just as we do. This happens not only with the ebb and flow of the seasons, when warm winter blankets are thrown on beds or screen doors are flung open, but also as our own needs change over time and our communities evolve. Perhaps this is why that feeling of "home" follows us from space to space as our street addresses change: While the outward expressions of our dwellings change form, their foundations—the people we share them with—stay the same.

Our homes are community builders. That community could consist of a life partner, a sprawling family, a collection of housemates or a humble party of one. Whatever form that community takes, our homes act as places where those people can come together and become closer. Forming our spaces with this in mind can strengthen the relationships that flourish under our roofs. The ways we choose to cultivate our communities are as varied as the assortments of people they support: It could mean hosting elaborate Saturday brunches for your friends or late-summer barbecues for your neighbors or savoring an indulgent dinner cross-legged on the floor, blissfully alone. It could mean knocking out a wall to open up your kitchen or adding walls for moments of private sanctuary. It could mean longer tables for longer evenings. It could mean anything that *means* something to you, really.

We set out to visit 35 diverse homes across five continents whose inhabitants embody these slow values through crafting homes that wholeheartedly express their own beliefs—they are our old friends, our new friends, our colleagues and our mentors. Instead of asking them to talk about the color of paint on their walls or the material they chose for their curtains, we invited them to share their values, how those ideals have shaped their homes and how their homes have in turn shaped them.

Although there are many iterations of the ways we can create slower lifestyles, we've divided this book into the three main features that these dwellings epitomize: homes that cultivate community, homes that simplify our lives and homes that allow us to live slowly and with intention. Each space encapsulates the spirit of all three, but we've allotted each home a chapter we feel best captures its family's principles, and we've also provided some in-depth reading material to elaborate on their messages.

We sincerely thank everyone involved for opening up their doors, their minds and often their pantries to show us how they approach and express slow living; it has been a pleasure.

The following residences may differ when it comes to their sizes, inhabitants, locations and aesthetics, but they all share one common denominator: Each of these homes is a vessel not for style, but for living. Welcome.

HOMES FOR COMMUNITY

Although home is often perceived as a private refuge, it can also be one of the most effective places to foster relationships—with those we live with, with friends we have over and with the community at large. Rather than merely sheltering us from the elements and holding all of our possessions, our homes are where we grow up, learn from our guardians, laugh with our friends, and argue (then make up) with our loved ones. A home's structure and the way we choose to fill it are major factors in these moments: A floor plan designed with community in mind might lead to longer conversations, more intimate memories and closer relationships. The homes and people featured in this chapter exemplify many different facets of community building—some prioritize personal growth while others nurture families; some open their doors to strangers as well as friends; and others are actively interwoven with their neighborhoods. At the core of all these community-minded homes is a shared understanding that the seemingly personal nature of the private home always nurtures more than one.

JOHN

& JULI BAKER

A single flight of stairs separates John and Juli Baker's business from their home environment. The founders of gallery and retail space Mjölk live with their young children, Elodie and Howell, in the bustling Junction neighborhood of Toronto, Canada. After purchasing a three-story Victorian building located on a busy thoroughfare, the couple enlisted the help of architects Peter Tan and Christine Ho Ping Kong of Studio Junction to consolidate the top two floors into a single-family home and transform the ground floor into a retail space. "We viewed them as collaborators who could take our ideas, expand on them and make them materialize," John says. Having their boutique and living quarters in the same building has made it surprisingly easy to balance work and family: John and Juli can switch between keeping an eye on the shop and carrying out various household duties, and Elodie loves popping downstairs to interact with customers. Locally sourced materials dominate the home's landscape, including Douglas fir floors, white oak cabinets and Quebec soapstone countertops in the kitchen. The cabinetry was made with wood instead of veneer and much of the stonework was left untreated so that the materials would improve with age. "The countertops show the most interesting patina effect because you can see where we tend to work: There are dark areas where our hands rest and where we cook. We think this adds life to the home," John says. "We're not striving for perfection, as that's impossible. We simply hope these natural materials show their value as they get more beautiful with age." Although their home was designed to be highly functional and accommodate their family's natural movements, John and Juli added a couple of "emotional elements" for enjoyment instead of efficiency, including a hinoki cedar bathtub they love to relax in after putting in long days at work. "Being able to soak in a wood tub after a hard day is a great stress reliever and will add some years to our lives," John says. "When we think of home, we don't just think in terms of functional interior design: The moments we have in that space with our family help to shape our ideas." An area that combines practicality with pleasure is their expansive third-floor courtyard that opens out to the sky and is separated from the house by glass windows. It's a nice substitute for a suburban backyard and gives the kids a safe space in which to run around and play. "Living in a city where we're constantly stimulated by noise and energy can feel overwhelming at times," John says. "Our home is a sanctuary away from the bustle of the city—a place to disconnect from the outside world and be safe to engage in the things that make us happy." By blending clean and efficient design with relaxing spaces, John and Juli have created an abode that will positively shape their work-life balance for years to come.

In the following essay on page 28, we consider the best ways to disconnect at the end of the day when your workplace and home are one and the same.

Above: The blue and white painting is by Junpei Ori. John and Juli are both fond of her work, which is inspired by Scandinavian culture and design.

Following Pages: Some of their favorite books to read to their young daughter, Elodie, are *Where the Wild Things Are* by Maurice Sendak, *The Paper Bag Princess* by Robert Munsch and Michael Martchenko and *There's No Such Thing as a Dragon* by Jack Kent.

Above: John has been studying the craft of Japanese tea ceremonies for some time. He uses a cast-iron kettle, an electric brazier, a *mizusashi* (clear water jar), a *kensui* (water container), a *chawan* (tea bowl) and a bamboo ladle to prepare the tea.

Right: Some of the couple's favorite culinary items include kitchenware designed by Oji Masanori and a copper and brass coffee dripper by Japanese company Hario.

WORDS : ANNE FULLERTON

BUILDING A
BALANCE

Switching off from work after hours is difficult when your office is also your living room. Reserving a time and space for other pursuits can help you focus on making the most of both work and play.

For those who work from home, maintaining a separation between the two ways of thinking can seem near impossible. Still, this hasn't stopped many from trying: Virginia Woolf kept a writing lodge at the bottom of her garden, Mark Twain wrote in a study so isolated from the rest of his house that his family had to summon him using a horn, and Norman Mailer went so far as to construct a "crow's nest" for writing in his Brooklyn town house—it was separated from the rest of the family residence by a three-story drop and accessible only via a gangplank.

This wasn't due to a lack of physical space: In all three cases, there was no shortage of rooms inside the houses where the authors could've chosen to write. Instead, it seems to hint at the desire for psychological space, a means of drawing a line—or, for Mailer, a vertigo-inducing chasm—between the professional and domestic spheres.

Because it's so tempting to view the lives of artists, writers, musicians, inventors, scientists or any of the greats exclusively through the lens of their work, we often forget that they also cultivated interests outside of their careers. Even those—or perhaps *especially* those—who are consumed by their craft need respite from it. Nowhere does this become more apparent than in the home.

For example, Woolf wasn't only a gifted novelist but also a nature lover with a keen eye for color. This was expressed in her writing through vivid descriptions of the natural world and also in the elaborate garden she tended with her husband at their Sussex home. She described their plot—complete with orchards and several greenhouses—as "the pride of their hearts." In 1920, she wrote that weeding produced "a queer sort of enthusiasm which made her say *this is happiness*."

On the other hand, Mailer was a sports fanatic eager to develop his own athleticism whenever he had the chance. His love of sailing was so great that he had his New York apartment remodeled in the image of a ship's cabin, complete with a hammock and rope ladders.

Meanwhile, Twain became legendary for his marathon billiards sessions, apparently dedicating up to nine hours a day to the game along with a significant amount of floor space in his Hartford home. He reportedly told a friend, "I walk not less than 10 miles every day with the cue in my hand." Having designed the house from scratch, he thought of the place less as a structure and more as another member of the family, writing, "To us, our house was not insentient matter—it had a heart, and a soul, and eyes to see us with."

While these writers' homes served in part as places to work, they also became places to retreat from it—spaces to nurture and practice the many other aspects of their lives.

Of course, we can't all afford to turn our homes into shrines to our interests: Budding sommeliers often have to forgo an underground cellar in favor of an IKEA closet full of wine crates, and would-be Julia Child protégés struggle with the logistics of serving a three-course meal on a one-square-foot coffee table. But the idea of creating an oasis in our homes—a place to escape from the daily grind—is one we can all strive for (even if our orchard is just a small window box, or our ship's cabin is a toy boat on the edge of the bathtub).

Ultimately, when we're able to switch off and leave our jobs at the door, we allow ourselves to put on our other hats—of friend, roommate, parent, partner, cook or gardener. These roles may not pay their share of the rent, and their audience may be smaller, but they're no less essential to who we are. When our house not only protects us from the elements but also fosters the many facets of our identity, that's when we know we're really, truly, home.

GERALDINE

CLEARY

When Geraldine Cleary asked Brisbane-based firm Donovan Hill Architects to build her home, she had no idea that their humble project—which has come to be known as the "D House"—would win the 2001 Robin Boyd Award, Australia's most prestigious residential architecture prize. "My house was intentionally designed to accommodate multiple configurations of relationships, activities and events, despite its modest scale," says Geraldine, a health and social policy researcher. She loves sharing her space with guests and frequently offers up her house as an inner-city venue for friends to host events. "Shared living is an important part of being operative in society and the world," she says. The house has accommodated various tenants over the years, including Timothy Hill—the lead architect of the D House—and her current lodger, the filmmaker and photographer Alex Chomicz. One of Geraldine's favorite aspects of her home is the interplay between the inside and the outside—this was achieved by designing the interior and exterior floor heights at the same exact level, extending certain materials to the outside realm and placing skylights above some interior walls, doors and parts of the kitchen, which allows these elements to be lit from above and cast shadows as if they were freestanding outdoor structures. "This creates continuity between the public and private territories, the

inside and outside areas, and the domestic and civic realms," Geraldine says. The high garden walls break down the breeze, light and sight lines so she can also treat the outside space like a room. "I furnish it with things you would normally associate with the interior of a house, such as flowers, upholstery and books, without them being blown around," she says. The interesting proportions of the house are highlighted by the use of scale: Smaller bedroom doors contrast with larger doors in the rest of the home, and the low and long window near the entrance creates the illusion that the wall it's set in is much bigger. "Some things are a bit too small and some are a bit too big, and the act of contrasting them engages the imagination," she says. Light also plays a huge role in creating the home's overall character—the house and its surfaces are oriented so the light that enters is reflected and therefore never too bright or harsh: The overall effect elevates the existing attributes of Geraldine's home. "The atmosphere of the house as a whole is calming, uplifting and comforting, and the changes in the light and shadows from morning to night and from one season to the next are sustaining," she says.

In the following essay on page 40, we explore why light has a positive influence on our homes, families and health.

Above Right: These ceramics were made by Melbourne-based designer Simon Lloyd. Geraldine received them as a gift from architect colleague John Wardle.

Right: The chairs on the far right of Geraldine's dining room were made by Danish furniture designer Hans Wegner.

Left: The large window that looks out onto the street is made of two sliding components: One is glazed glass and the other is a timber screen. Geraldine often has the screen closed with the glass open on summer evenings, but she slides everything open for parties.

WORDS : GEORGIA FRANCES KING

LETTING IN
THE LIGHT

When it comes to the essentials for a happy living environment, having a home flooded with natural light is often at the top of our lists. By tweaking just a few small aspects of our daily rituals, we can improve our relationship with the sun to benefit both our homes and our health.

Every day presents us with all kinds of decisions to make about our lifestyles, and there are plenty of self-diagnosis websites, new age books and mothers-in-law ready to indisputably instruct us on the choices we should be making. In an attempt to better ourselves, we try to obey their mantras: We sleep eight hours a night; we opt for whole grains instead of white flour; we drag our reluctant bodies out for a quick jog; we choose not to open the second bottle of Riesling. But what if there were something more vital affecting our health? One that predated gluten alternatives and spin classes?

For the past few billion years, the sun has reliably risen every morning and set every evening. Our bodies have therefore come to expect its daily spiral through the sky, and most of our biological systems work on the assumption that we'll follow along with its sunlight-based sequence. But now instead of waking with dawn, we have snooze buttons. Instead of dozing at dusk, we have Netflix.

Sunlight plays an intrinsic role in our lives and has a profound effect on the way we think and how our bodies function. Through its role guiding our circadian rhythms—the internal clocks that keep us regulated—sunlight can control everything from our sleeping habits to our wintertime melted-cheese cravings. By making small changes in both our routines and our homes, we can help our bodies stay in sync.

But how did we lose our connection to sunlight in the first place? Were we complicit in our demise into dimness? When Thomas Edison popularized the lightbulb some 135 years ago, he was unwittingly ending our close relationship with natural light: Thanks to the humble lightbulb, we can now work graveyard shifts and salsa until dawn. Convenience glowed brighter than our biological clocks, and we've been slowly letting them fall out of sync ever since.

By synchronizing ourselves and our homes with the sun, we may be able to reconnect with the undulation of the day and its restorative power. Here are some quick ways to fine-tune your light-related habits:

Don't Hide Behind Glass

They say that people who live in glass houses shouldn't throw stones, but they should throw open a window: Just like sunscreen helpfully blocks our skin from certain harmful light frequencies, the glass in windows deflects some other frequencies our bodies need to trigger biological responses. It's handy that we don't burn while sitting in a sunlit living room all day, but the fact we don't scorch should be a clue that we're not getting all that the sun has to offer. If your home is already configured to let in a lot of light, consider opening a window and basking in it—you'll soak up more vitamin D without a pane of glass getting in the way.

Observe Dawn and Dusk Outside

Instead of sipping your morning coffee on the couch while the sun is rising, wrap yourself in something warm and perch outside. While there's plenty left to learn, it's becoming apparent that dawn and dusk may be the most important parts of the day for us to be outdoors in order to help set our circadian rhythms: The light quality at these times is changing rapidly, and that change is absorbed by our eyes and translated by our brains to serve as a biological cue for whether it's early or late, thereby orienting our cells to wake up or fall asleep. These effects are best felt by being outside when the sky slowly turns from black to blue and back again. By getting up 20 minutes earlier to walk the dog at dawn or snacking on charcuterie while watching the sun set from your porch, you could be helping your body work out if it should be revving up or winding down.

Black Out Your Bedroom

Sleeping eight hours a night is beneficial, but not if our bodies think it's daytime. Switching on the bathroom light or checking emails in a bout of insomnia might not be the biggest problem either—the most disruptive factor may be the ambient light pollution drifting in through your windows. To counter this effect, you can either block your windows with heavy curtains or wear a very chic sleep mask—at least no one will be able to see you in the dark.

When it comes to aligning yourself and your home with the light, the most important factor is figuring out what works best for you—even the act of being conscious about sunlight is a step in the right direction. As time goes on and the sun continues to rise and set every day until it flickers out, we will continue to learn how to have a better relationship with it. There's still so much to discover, but at least we're beginning to see the light.

YVONNE KONÉ

& RASMUS JUUL

Yvonne Koné and Rasmus Juul moved to the Copenhagen suburb of Vesterbro a decade ago because they were inspired by its rich history and historic atmosphere. The apartment building they currently live in with their children—Johanna, Bror and Hasse—was built in the 19th century by the Art Nouveau–inspired architect Anton Rosen and offers a welcomed respite from the rest of the city. "This is where I relax completely with no filters," Yvonne says. She and her husband, a children's book illustrator, have watched their neighborhood shift over the years (a recent influx of residents has brought a new mix of families, professionals and young newcomers), and Yvonne feels like both she and their home are changing along with it. "I like things in movement and the feeling that nothing is static," she says. With half of her brain leaning toward perfectionism and the other half toward what she describes as complete disorganization, the couple's home is usually redecorated at least once a year. "Painting the walls has always given me the feeling of a fresh start—it's like a clean canvas," she says. "I'm not very attached to physical things, and when I'm redecorating as often as I do, I see it more as a form of exchanging rather than consuming—

I sell some items and then find a few more." Whenever she redecorates, Yvonne tries to make the decor minimal and manageable, as having three children and a time-consuming job as a designer keeps her busy as it is. She and Rasmus are fans of their home's foundation of smooth, clean walls combined with pinewood floors, but she says, "The perfectionist in me has accepted that it's OK for there to be a little—or sometimes a very big—mess." The duo also believes that a resident's personality should be clearly visible in their space. "After looking at a few items in a home, you can tell that someone selected a particular piece for a reason—not necessarily because it was beautiful, but simply because someone liked it," she says. A possession that speaks to this notion is a set of warm, plush bathrobes that Yvonne gave to the family members for Christmas a few years ago. Along with lighting some flickering candles, wearing the robes has become a household tradition during the dark Danish winters when they function as the family's around-the-clock loungewear. While the robes aren't fancy ("Rasmus thinks they're kind of sloppy," she says, laughing), they exemplify a sense of comfort that she hopes to keep throughout her home.

Left: Yvonne designed the couch in the living room, the rug is a handwoven Berber carpet from Morocco and the coffee table was found at a thrift store in Italy. Her son, Bror, created the drawings displayed on the windowsill.

Above: The chair in the kitchen is by Danish brand Please Wait To Be Seated. Rasmus enjoys whipping up meals for the family, especially dishes that remind them of their trips to Greece.

Above Left: Yvonne's favorite sketchbooks are made by the Copenhagen design company L.A. Graphic Design.

Right: The couple's children love the spacious feel of the apartment. Rasmus is an avid collector of art books and drew most of the sketches on their bookshelves.

KHAI LIEW

& NICHOLE

PALYGA

Many of designer and curator Khai Liew's fondest memories of home are rooted in his childhood residence in Malaysia, which his father built in 1964. "There was a sense of beautiful proportion to the house," Khai says. "Everything about how it sat on the land felt right: The way my father carved out the space instilled a sense of volume and proportion in me." At age 18, Khai moved to Adelaide, Australia, where he currently lives with his partner, Nichole Palyga. "We've worked together for more than 10 years. Khai designs and I manage the practice, though the roles constantly overlap," Nichole says. Khai's formative years as a collector and conservator of early Australian furniture and folk art piqued his interest in the distinctive quality and sense of permanence offered by various types of solid wood, which led the couple to furnish their living space with predominantly wood-based textures. Coupled with the "fortress-like feel" of the home's exterior, these materials provide the reassurance, security and privacy Khai identifies with being at home. "Our house is an orderly one where everything has a place," he says. "Each time I open the front door, I can sense the tranquility." One of the couple's favorite areas is the central indoor courtyard, which brings light and a sense of

space to the house. Khai cooks in the courtyard all year round, so it's very much an additional living area. "The light there is especially beautiful on a late summer evening," he says. "It takes on a magical and intense bluish-gray tone, and its calming effect permeates the whole house." Khai's work as a curator has trained him to be meticulous and disciplined about what he brings into their personal space—objects are carefully selected and placed alongside each other to create a dialogue in the area where they sit. "The result is harmonious, and in the harmony there is calm and stillness," he says. Items made by the couple's friends are also interspersed with Khai's own work: His designs are heavily influenced by his eclectic cultural experiences and tell stories about his Chinese-Malay childhood and other groups who have migrated to Australia. "I find inspiration in the slightest silhouette, the fold of a skirt, the face of a Japanese bride in traditional dress, the weave in a basket, the flow of Islamic calligraphy or a dancer's pose, to name a few," he says.

In the following essay on page 64, Khai elaborates on how his multicultural upbringing has influenced his approach to design.

Left: The Adelaide-based artist Helen Fuller, who is a friend of Khai's, designed the ceramic vases. Nichole picked up the teak box on a trip to Copenhagen, and the teak chair is by an unknown mid-century Danish designer. André Derain painted the artwork on the wall.

Above: A 1930s Japanese gown hangs from the couple's headboard. The abacus is a piece of 19th-century Australian folk art. Khai designed both the American walnut bedside table and the lamp with a mulberry-bark paper shade.

Above: The two paintings are by Danish painter Johannes Hof-meister and the candlestick holders are by Jens Quistgaard. Khai made the dining table out of European oak and the chairs were designed by Niels and Eva Koppel.

Above Right: The triptych on the wall is by Khai's friend Jessica Loughlin, a glass artist. Khai designed the chest of drawers and suspects that the easy chair—which has no maker's stamp on it—is a rare prototype by Jens Quistgaard.

WORDS : KHAI LIEW

DOMESTIC
INTERSECTIONS

Designer Khai Liew's Australian home is a space where nostalgia, folk art and contemporary components coexist. Shaped by his upbringing in Kuala Lumpur, Malaysia, Khai's multicultural influences are evident in both his personal and professional aesthetics.

Home is where I can feel at peace, where freedom can be found and where my memories are. I've lived in the beautiful city of Adelaide my entire adult life. I arrived in Australia as a bright-eyed teenager eager to take on new experiences alone in a far-off land. Although the transition posed its challenges, I found happiness and comfort in my new surroundings almost instantly thanks to the strolling distance between my school and the beach. It was like settling into an endless summer, all fish-and-chips and burning feet on hot sand.

I tend to surround myself with things that reflect my history, my encounters and my friendships. My most prized possession is a silk-lined winter jacket that my mother made for me when I first left Kuala Lumpur for Adelaide at age 18. I was brought up in year-round tropical heat, so I had absolutely no notion of the implications of winter. She knew the jacket would be more than something to keep me warm—it also served as a conduit to family memories. Some 20 years later, she mended its worn cloth with much care, keeping both the object and the memories intact.

I'm very disciplined with what I bring into our home. For many years I collected, conserved and dealt in early Australian furniture and folk art, so I've spent a lifetime assessing works of great merit and living with them. I surround myself with objects made by good friends—mostly artists working in Adelaide—interspersed with some of my own designs. I'm good at distilling what I don't want and I'm happy to live with less. I like to group items from different disciplines as if they were conversing, bound by the visual language shared by the artists whose work I collect. These pieces are carefully selected and represent much more than mere decoration: They're in our house not only because they enrich our lives aesthetically, but also because they're full of rich meaning.

The meaning behind objects and design is intrinsic to my own practice. I like to tell stories with my furniture designs, such as the 19th-century European migration to Australia or tales of my upbringing in Malaysia. Collaborating with fellow artists brings about a wonderful confluence of ideas and fresh dialogues that explore aspects of the Asian diaspora and the historical, sociological, cultural and physical facets of the Australian landscape.

Although it's been many years since I left Malaysia, the experiences I had in my childhood home remain a great influencer to this day. In 1964, my father built a Japanese-inspired house atop a hill overlooking Kuala Lumpur. As a child, I loitered around the building site watching the joiners and carpenters use hand tools to fabricate the floorboards, *shōji* sliding doors and beautiful wooden cupboards, and I imagined how I'd furnish it—I was already busily dreaming and designing. Although there were 11 of us who lived there, it felt like a quiet house. It now occurs to me that my father achieved this by balancing the mass of the house with the employment of negative space, which is the core idea behind the Japanese concept of *ma*.

This blend of mid-century modernism, the spirit of the Japanese aesthetic and the importance of space, light and materials has always stayed with me. I strongly subscribe to the notions of both sensual design and architecture that places an emphasis on textured natural materials, habitableness and the right light. Wood is everywhere in our house— each piece of furniture feels different and has a distinct smell. The mark of the hand is evident in almost all the things that I live with or make for the house: Whether it's a porcelain spoon, a wooden ladle or a dining chair, I appreciate that a direct link to the maker can be found through craftsmanship.

JESSICA

DE RUITER

& JED LIND

Jessica de Ruiter and Jed Lind's neighborhood provides the perfect back-drop for their relaxed California lifestyle. The former East Coasters live in Silver Lake, Los Angeles, in a 1953 Gregory Ain–designed home with their daughter, James, and an Australian shepherd named Blue. "We love the strong sense of community in our neighborhood and the pride its residents take in all aspects of living here," says Jessica, a fashion editor and stylist. "It's filled with a nice mix of young families, creative types and people who've been here for generations and have seen it go through immense change over the years." The family often begins its day with a hike around the Silver Lake reservoir and also visits the running trails, meadows and playgrounds close by. "We like how it's a bit tucked away from the craziness of the rest of Los Angeles, so coming home at the end of the day feels like a retreat," says Jed, an interior designer. Their affection for the sunshine and outdoors extends to their home, where they've created a seamless flow between the interior and exterior. They also love the way their house was constructed to accommodate the changing sunlight throughout the day: The windows are smaller on the side of the house where the sun rises so it doesn't disturb the residents, but the floor-to-ceiling windows on the opposite walls let in generous views of the sunset. "We get some amazing golden-hour panoramas

from our living room," she says. Although the property was initially constructed as an artist's residence and needed a fair bit of renovation to suit a family's needs, they were mindful of respecting the home's original design. "We knew that we needed to update the place, but we wanted to restore rather than renovate," Jessica says. "Gregory Ain's daughter actually made an impromptu visit during our renovations and told us her father would've been proud of what we've done, which was a really special affirmation." Jessica and Jed describe themselves as "intensely visual" people whose creative backgrounds have greatly influenced their decorating choices, from the unique furniture they've amassed over the years to the art hanging on the walls. Much of their collection was inherited from Jed's late mother, who was a keen art collector, while other pieces were acquired from trades with Jed's artist friends. "Jessica is definitely more traditional and classic in her taste, and I veer more toward modern minimal design," Jed says. "But we both gravitate to timeless design in both interiors and fashion and prefer to invest in pieces that are going to be with us forever."

In the following essay on page 76, we take a cue from Jessica and Jed's morning hikes to discover how other creatives spend the day's earliest hours.

Above Right: James likes to host tea parties for her stuffed animals. Jed made the table and assembled the chairs from various trips to the flea market.

Following Page: These fluid ceramic pieces were designed by local artist David Korty.

This is a certificate for Rirkrit Tiravanija's
Untitled (lunch box), 1996.

- 4 level Rocket Brand stainless steel food
  container (4 x 16)
- Bangkok newspaper
- A meal as listed in the following menu

Menu: หมูสะเต๊ะ
        pork satay
        ส้มตำ
        green papaya salad
        แกงกะหรี่ไก่
        chicken yellow curry
        ข้าว
        rice

42/108

Left: Elad Lassry took the photograph hanging on the wall and the potted plant is a New Zealand laurel. Some of Jessica's favorite linen brands include Frette, C&C Milano, Rogers & Goffigon, Matteo and Loro Piana.

Above: Although Jessica and Jed are huge fans of the cinder block and exposed aggregate in their backyard, Jed decided to soften it by planting roses, lavender and olive trees and added beds of boxwood around the pool.

Following Pages: Jessica loves these photographs taken by the Los Angeles artist John Divola. For this series, he went out into the Mojave Desert and took photos of wild dogs while they chased his car.

WORDS : MARGARET EVERTON

BEFORE THE
DAY STARTS

Making the most of the morning's predawn hours can be the best way to start the day, whether they're used for reading, ruminating or romanticizing. By harnessing the time that passes before the rest of the world rises, we can jump-start both our days and our minds.

Early mornings are dark and quiet. Although your warm bed beckons you to climb back in, starting your day *before* the day can leave you feeling enlightened and ready to meet life's forthcoming requirements that rise with the sun. It's not a time to get ahead at work or skim your social-media feed—those can wait, as can the laundry, the shopping list and the call to your mom. These things will get done, but the early morning hours offer you a chance to do something for yourself and should therefore be protected.

Countless early birds have refused to let menial daily tasks bully this golden time. Before entering her studio for the day, Georgia O'Keeffe woke at dawn to the sound of her dogs barking, warmed up with tea and then took a walk. Henry David Thoreau ventured out into the frigid morning to hear the first birdsongs. While his wife slept in, P.G. Wodehouse did calisthenics on his front porch before reading pop fiction over coffee cake, toast and tea.

Others rose early to pursue their passions before beginning their normal life. Sylvia Plath woke at 5 a.m. to write before caring for her two young children, as did Toni Morrison, who raised her two sons while working in a publishing house. ("It's not being *in* the light," she said. "It's being there *before it arrives*.") His days filled with business, Frank Lloyd Wright developed his architectural designs from 4 to 7 a.m., and Immanuel Kant meditated over a pipe and weak tea before heading to the local university to teach science.

Rising at the same time every day can establish a ritual (plus the consistency helps prevent you from giving up). Whether you wake up early to work on a passion project or use that time to indulge in doing nothing, beginning with a routine makes these moments distinct. The night before, prepare your French press or set out your loose-leaf tea so all you have to do in the morning is stumble into the kitchen and blearily boil water. Listen to Glenn Gould's version of Bach's *Goldberg Variations*—or Daft Punk, if you prefer. Or if you crave a more ascetic start, put on a sweater and slink over to you desk without a sound. The morning may be cold, but you'll warm up as you awaken and devote a fresh and unadulterated mind to your fascinations.

But what if you can't rouse yourself despite your best intentions? Perhaps you push the snooze button incessantly or decide that no amount of predawn enlightenment is worth the lull you fall into by mid-afternoon. Thankfully, the fullness of life is not proportionate to how early you rise. Proust slept during the day and worked through the night, George Gershwin came home after evening parties to compose music until dawn, and George Sand often left her lovers' beds to write in the midnight silence that inspired her.

Whether their gravitational pull was toward morning or night, these visionaries all established a daily space for themselves only and refused to let their creative spirits hibernate along with the sun. Their efforts were both large and small, but always deliberate. If all you do is wake up 15 minutes earlier to sip rather than gulp your coffee, you're opening yourself up to a more intimate life. As the German idiom goes, "The early morning has gold in its mouth." And who doesn't want to be dusted with gold?

DELCY MORELOS

& GABRIEL

SIERRA

Artists Delcy Morelos and Gabriel Sierra have transformed their home into a gallery of their own with stacks of books, inspiration boards and sculptures covering most available surfaces—but their style of arranging is intentional and shouldn't be confused with clutter. "Everything we own has to be useful or at least have an important symbolic meaning," Gabriel says. "Objects must be arranged by following the geometry of the space, which is shaped by the architecture." Living in the bustling neighborhood of Las Aguas in Colombia's capital of Bogotá, the couple has carved out and carefully created a nest amid the surrounding government buildings and offices. "Our apartment is a kind of sanctuary where we escape from the world," Gabriel says. He and Delcy and have lived in this apartment with their four pets—cats Bacalao and Ratón and dogs Sopa and Plato—since 2001, but the building has been standing since the 1930s. Some of the structure's history may have even unconsciously influenced their decorative choices. "Sometimes we think our home is composed of information and memories from other houses we knew in previous lives or in parallel universes," he says. When they moved in,

the duo didn't do any major renovations beyond painting the doors and cupboards with white enamel to help brighten up the space. Instead, they focused primarily on making the space more functional and comfortable by adding bookshelves, tables and chairs to match their needs. Accepting the inescapability of an artist's never-ending work cycle, they also chose to integrate a workspace into their home: Gabriel has a room inside the apartment for smaller projects like drawing and model-making, and Delcy has a larger studio on the ground floor of the building for her projects. When they need a break, the artists journey out from the facade of their unassuming dark brick building for a walk in the vibrant city center. But they also enjoy spending a lot of time simply pondering and relaxing at home. "I believe the house is an important layer of our personalities through which we discover and dwell in the physical world," Gabriel says.

In the following essay on page 90, we consider the importance of setting aside time to do nothing except stare out the window.

FIRST QUALITY

Above Right: A wooden architecture model, an old natural
history book and a figurine found at a Bogotá flea market sit on
a small table. The larger chair is an Eames design.

204-205. *Tim Mapston, Sculpture III, 1974.*

Previous Pages: Gabriel created the wood screen with a carpenter friend using cloth hinges. It was originally going to be part of an art project, but he ended up using it to divide the living room area from the couple's library. The images on the walls are a combination of old postcards and pictures found in newspapers, magazines and books.

Above Right: Delcy works on a piece of artwork in her studio, which is in the same building as their apartment.

WORDS : NIKAELA MARIE PETERS

A ROOM
WITH A VIEW

Our homes are often where we unwind by actively puttering around—
cooking, gardening, decorating—but it's also important to take time
to gaze out the window and enjoy doing nothing at all.

Seven years ago, I lived in an apartment without an internet connection and a flip phone that worked only to make calls and send 40-character texts. My bedroom had a third-story view of a busy downtown street; it was small, and the bed was pushed up against the window. I'm sure the hours I spent staring out that window would have added up to weeks of time. Without the distraction of the internet or the option of watching a movie, I was certainly more productive, according to certain measures. I watched nothing and anything outside. I drank coffee and (occasionally) smoked cigarettes—two habits that while unhealthy for the body can, in certain circumstances, have health benefits for the soul.

A mind adrift in a sea of its own making is far more interesting than a mind following a trail of hyperlinks. But when I compare those years to now, what strikes me as a greater loss is all the time I spent doing *nothing*. It's the stuff of gods and infants—the birthplace of great works of art, philosophy and science. The habit of doing nothing at all is incredibly important to our individual and cultural well-being, yet it seems to be dying in our digitized age.

Far from laziness, proper idleness is the soul's home base. Before we plan or love or act or storytell, we are idle. Before we learn, we watch. Before we do, we dream. Before we play, we imagine. The idle mind is awake but unconstrained, free to slip untethered from idea to idea or meander from potential theory to potential truth. Philosopher and friar St. Thomas Aquinas argued, "It is necessary for the perfection of human society that there should be men who devote their lives to contemplation." That third-story apartment window enabled such rumination.

When a view is familiar, we can look without registering much at all. On the other hand, because it's familiar, we know it intimately and are able to register, perhaps by osmosis, the details that others would miss. We perceive the small changes: the first chickadee, the white-brown-green-brown of the year, the new hedge across the street. The window is for distracting ourselves while simultaneously paying careful attention. Both of these opposites enable each other. Author Karl Ove Knausgård noted there's a strange comfort in "taking notice of the world while we pass through it, [all the while] the world taking no notice of us."

Is true idleness a lost skill? How often do we sit serenely unoccupied? How often do we walk, as Henry David Thoreau advised, with no agenda or destination, present and free? What an uncommon sight: a solitary individual, his head not buried in a newspaper or laptop or phone, simply sitting—his mind long wandered off.

Productivity is not the only measure of time well spent. Some of the most important scientific innovations and inventions were "happened upon," unplanned, after years of unproductive, leisurely puzzling. My five-month-old understands this intuitively: He'll learn an entire language and how to sit, stand, crawl and walk all by doing mostly what may look like nothing to an adult.

The time we spend idle makes for a healthier state of mind. Simpler things bring us joy. We want less and are more at peace when we get it. We sleep better and work harder. When we observe our immediate surroundings, we are more grounded in our context and more attuned to the rhythms of whatever season or home we are in.

NATHALIE

SCHWER

For stylist Nathalie Schwer, entertaining is inextricably linked to her home's identity. "I love the freedom of being able to host people and that my house has become a familiar base to many of my friends," she says. Hosting gatherings gives Nathalie an opportunity to experiment with cooking different vegetarian meals, and her guests often show up ready to pitch in or bring a delicious offering of their own. "I don't usually follow recipes," she says. "I prefer to invent dishes on the spot while I'm shopping for groceries. I'm constantly testing out these creations on my friends." The Danes love socializing indoors as a natural response to the cold weather and short daylight hours, and Nathalie particularly enjoys opening her home to friends during the winter months: She makes sure there's plenty of firewood and tea on hand for her guests to while away the evening hours around her fireplace. "Danish people really know how to cope with and structure their activities around the weather," she says. "Starting in September, you'll often hear people say they're looking forward to the opportunity to hang out inside." Nathalie, who has lived on her own since she was 18, calls a spacious apartment by the waterfront home. Her neighborhood of Islands Brygge is a close-knit community where she's come to know the people who live around her, such as the local merchants and shopkeepers, and the beautiful setting only makes it feel even more special. "I have an open view and so much greenery around my home, and it's wonderful to observe how the character of the city changes with the seasons," she says. When it comes to decorating,

Nathalie treats her living space like a workshop and gives herself the freedom to frequently change the layout and furniture in her home. This allows her to experiment and think creatively. "It's become a bit of a joke within my circle of friends and family, but I love that my house isn't so delicate that I'm nervous to switch things up," she says. "It's like a grown-up playground for my creativity and ideas." Nathalie's work brings her into contact with many different stylists, designers and artists, so her home gives her a space to display the eclectic mix of objects and collectibles she's accumulated through her job. Some of her favorite items include her grandmother's couch, a hi-fi stereo and the various art pieces she's collected over the years. "At least 90 percent of my furniture is stuff that I've inherited or received as gifts or was made by friends, so I guess my decorating style is pretty sentimental," Nathalie says. "It means a lot to me to be surrounded by items with history—either because they've been passed down through my family or created specially by close acquaintances or because I've somehow fallen for the soul of the object." Nathalie is a firm believer in bucking interior-design trends in favor of staying true to what feels comfortable and organic to the space and the person living in it, and she stresses the importance of personal style and authenticity. "Objects in the home should be a natural extension of the resident's lifestyle—otherwise they'll feel strange and out of place," she says. "It's kind of like wearing a huge dress when going to play soccer—it just doesn't function all that well."

Left: Nathalie's Frama wall light serves both as a lamp and as a small bedside table. She loves reading in bed and is currently perusing *Beyond* by Dan Graham. A Rodin sketch and a picture of a mountain she found at a flea market are on the wall.

Above: Nathalie's wallpaper is by Farrow & Ball, a traditional English paint and wallpaper company.

Above: Nathalie's vintage table is a type that was once traditionally used in Danish kitchens, and her lamp is also vintage. She enjoys decorating her house with various plants from her local florist.

Following Page: The artwork on Nathalie's wall is a print by American painter Mark Rothko and she found her vintage coffee table at a Comme des Garçons pop-up store. Her morning routine involves drinking two large cups of coffee and listening to talk shows on her dad's old radio from the '70s.

MICHAEL

ELMGREEN

& INGAR DRAGSET

Since their creative partnership began in 1995, contemporary artists Michael Elmgreen and Ingar Dragset have based their collaborations on breaking down the barriers between public and private spaces. "The conventional notion of what's considered public and private is a social construct that we've inherited from past generations and needs to be constantly reevaluated," Michael says. When they saw an advertisement for a water pumping station in Berlin's Neukölln neighborhood 10 years ago, they adopted this concept while developing their own uniquely structured space. For years, the building sat unclaimed on an unassuming residential street adjacent to a small overgrown meadow covering the former reservoir behind it. It had remained empty because no one could imagine how to appropriate such a large space in a non-industrial location—that is, until Michael and Ingar found it. "We were looking for a place that could meet many different needs, such as workshops, office space, archival space, living space and social space," Michael says. After purchasing the sprawling warehouse-like structure, they renovated and divided the building into a number of different zones to be used for domestic life, work and socializing. "On a typical day here, there can be up to a dozen people working on different projects and eating lunch together in the kitchen," Ingar says. "We also have a number of guest rooms and some more domestic-looking areas where we have

meetings. Flexibility is key." Although the former couple both lived here for many years, Michael currently splits his time between London and Berlin, and the space now operates primarily as the main studio for their artistic practice under the name Elmgreen & Dragset. Their staff works from various areas in the building and seasonally shifts between the open main floor in the summer and a smaller winter office to keep warm, as a building this large is notoriously difficult to heat. Features such as the main hall's 42-foot (13-meter) ceiling are used to create full-scale mock-ups for installation pieces, and the front doors swing open so crated artwork can be moved into and out of the studio. Michael and Ingar have filled the rooms with a lot of their furniture from past shows and art projects. These items serve as a constant reminder of the evolution of both their space and their artistic practice. "When we use furniture in our exhibitions, it's chosen to convey a certain emotion. When it leaves the context of the exhibition space and is used in our home, the functionality usually remains, but the meaning slightly shifts," Ingar says. "After all, there's a good portion of ourselves in any of the characters we invent for our projects."

In the following interview on page 108, the artists talk more about their work as Elmgreen & Dragset and the nature of public and private space.

Left: This Henrik Olesen photograph is one of Michael and Ingar's favorite pieces. The ceramics are initial prototypes of a few of their artworks, and they collaborated with Wenk and Wiese, the architecture firm that renovated their building, to design the fireplace.

Above Right: These photos are from the 2005 Elmgreen & Dragset project "Deutsche Museen." They asked a number of German museums to send representational images of their exhibition spaces when empty. Eight images were selected, manipulated and printed as photogravures.

Left: Michael and Ingar's warehouse space covers nearly 11,000 square feet (1,000 square meters). These bookshelves contain their entire press archive over the past two decades, which includes magazines and publications dating from the mid-'90s to the present.

PUBLIC
ACCESS

*Elmgreen & Dragset are an artistic duo known for turning gallery spaces
into illusions of private homes, complete with dirty dishes left in the sink.
They discuss what happens when private homes and public spaces intersect
and what it's taught them about crafting their own living quarters.*

What messages about the blurry line between public and private space are you trying to explore through your art? — We're interested in how the function of public space has changed over the past few decades and how its role has been displaced within our contemporary digitized culture. Many interactions—such as socializing and exchanging opinions—used to take place in public spaces but now take place online. Today politicians and urban planners seem to regard public space as a problem that needs to be solved, rather than recognizing its potential for creating new social platforms. We try to look more deeply into whose stories get to be told and what viewpoints are being presented. In some of our projects, we've also explored what kinds of power structures are in place in both public and private spheres and what desire mechanisms guide our behavioral patterns or dictate how we experience public designs and architecture. We've also worked with simple structural alterations of spaces in order to show how easy it can be to twist the conventional use of a specific place, whether it's a museum, a gallery or a public square.

Your home contains many different spaces that are both publicly accessible and private. How have you learned to separate your personal lives from the work you do with your team at home? — We have some communal areas that are accessible to everyone and some areas that are more private, though never completely. Nothing is formally mapped out, and we try not to have any specific rules in the space. There's a sort of unspoken general understanding between all of us at the studio about where everyone goes and when. For example, the main hall is always open to everyone as it's also where we produce many of our works, as is the kitchen, which has many different functions and is sort of a central meeting point. The upstairs area is understood to be more private—on a typical day, the studio staff doesn't go upstairs unless the weekly yoga class is taking place or there's some special meeting or guests are visiting. It's the quietest part of the building. We also all have lunch in the garden together in the summer.

When decorating our homes, do you think we should make decisions based purely on our personal preferences or be mindful of what those objects say about us? — You should make decisions based on personal preferences, for sure. We shouldn't be ashamed of showing our desires, perversions, neurosis or banalities. A home should be a place that reflects your personal taste—an environment that's crafted by the inhabitant.

The residents in your home-based exhibitions are nearly always absent, leaving us to conclude what types of people they are from their belongings. What do you think the belongings in your own home say about you? — You could say that putting these spaces on display highlights the urgency of having a private sphere—a place where we dare to be ourselves, with all our obsessions and phobias, without being judged or watched. The objects in the studio reflect many things—our weird passions, our inspirations and our cultural backgrounds as Scandinavians. For instance, we're always reading, and our custom-built bookshelves upstairs hold a wide range of titles that have influenced our work: There are books on gay culture, performance art, philosophy and architecture, as well as theoretical essays on public space, among other things. Most of the artwork you see on our walls is from friends. A lot of the pieces of furniture are relics from previous exhibitions or vintage stuff we've bought at markets or in secondhand stores. And a few designs we've made ourselves because we couldn't find what we were looking for.

What has living in a semipublic setting taught you about yourselves? — The studio layout has definitely been instrumental in reshaping our working method, and we've learned that this kind of semipublic setting can create new rhythms of productivity and encourage us to cross some borders. It's been important for both of us to overcome our own shyness and dare to show things that are still in progress—things that might not appear visually optimal yet. Having more public exposure in our private sphere teaches us to be less fearful and less vain.

How do you think our attitudes toward opening up our private spaces to strangers are changing? — Airbnb—along with social-media sites such as Facebook and Instagram—has played a big part in shifting attitudes toward opening up not only our private spaces but also our intimate moments to strangers. It's becoming quite normal to display more and more parts of our lives online: It's a new way of profiling yourself for the world and forming a carefully crafted identity.

What's the relationship between architecture and public art? Should our homes' exteriors be treated as works of art? — No, too much architecture is already reduced to its exterior—buildings that are only skin with no organs. Public art projects should be more architectural instead; something that could be inhabited would be far more interesting.

AURÉLIE LÉCUYER & JEAN CHRISTOPHE

The timeworn features of Aurélie Lécuyer and Jean Christophe's house make their family feel at home. "We love places that have a story, a past—places where materials tell you something special," Aurélie says. The couple recently bought an apartment in Nantes, a beautiful city in western France, in a building that dates back to the early 1900s. Both inside and out, their home's environment has the casual energy and ease of a bygone era: Hallways are filled with the sounds of their three children —Gustave, Honoré and Blanche—playing, and everything they need is accessible by foot, from their school to the market and the local cinema. The combination of the area's storied history and the constant activity in and around their home often reminds Aurélie of the fluidity of domestic life. "I can't imagine a finished home," she says. "We think about it all the time, and it can't be static. A home is permanently evolving, just as children do and as we do. It's quite impossible to keep something frozen in time here." As a stylist, Aurélie sees every element of an interior as a contributing factor to the tale being told by a decorator. "Depending on the objects we collect and the conversations they start together, there are so many stories that come to life in a home," she says. The couple believes the whole structure is a moving organism that reflects its inhabitants' narratives—as each family member's passions and personal tastes change, so does their home. "The materials, colors, forms and the added tiny little details tell their own stories. Each creates its own universe," Aurélie says. She and Jean believe the space you create is meant to foster a sense of relief from external daily pressures. But as everyone's desires and whims are different—especially with three kids—they think it's important that each member of the family has a designated private space, a "kind of personal cocoon." Providing a personal universe for each family member gives everybody the opportunity to relax away from the nonstop hustle of household life. For her own purposes, Aurélie added a separate workspace in the master bedroom. "The apartment isn't that big, but it's always quiet there even when it's not in the rest of the house," she says. "That's enough for me—a quiet space and an outside view." But despite her dedication to finding a personal place within the home, Aurélie still enjoys absorbing inspiration from her family for her work. "Clothes from Blanche's wardrobe help me set up colors, Honoré's drawings are placed on my inspiration boards and Gustave's rigor shows me how to organize myself," she says.

In the following essay on page 118, we consider how children change both the meaning and the function of a home.

Above: Aurélie finds pictures in magazines, frames them and then hangs them up on her children's walls. The tree wallpaper is by Swedish brand Sandberg.

Following Page: Aurélie and Jean's vintage sofa was designed by Michel Ducaroy for Ligne Roset in 1973.

Previous Page: Aurélie discovered these wooden shelves at a vintage store. Her son Gustave loves his collection of toy cars—his grandfather gave him some, and his parents pick up others for him when traveling.

Above: The couple found this cowhide rug at a flea market and the mobile is by the Toronto-based brand Bookhou.

WORDS : MARGARET EVERTON

THE KIDS
ARE ALL RIGHT

Welcoming children into a home means more than just spaghetti stains on the carpet and plastic dinosaurs scattered on the stairs: Kids can also help us define our homes, teach us what's truly important and encourage us to let the meaningless nonessentials slide.

Having kids doesn't just change a home—it revolutionizes it. When children are introduced, the dwelling undergoes a metamorphosis, and each parent needs to find a new way to live and share as they cross the threshold into an otherworldly terrain brimming with a mysterious and intoxicating energy.

When children are added to a home, the change is palpable. Olive forks become tridents for a miniature Viking ship. An uneven heart is etched into the leg of a once-flawless antique end table. Pots and pans are now percussion, sippy cups get stacked with the teacups and the hallway is scribbled pink after a toddler took your "wanting more color in the house" remark literally. You start to find things in unusual places, like the horse figurine inside the empty French press or a raisin smashed onto the piano's middle C key. Others are inexplicably lost: the strap from your handbag, a Rolling Stones' *Aftermath* record, half of the soupspoons. A living room that remains perfectly tidy for more than 30 minutes becomes a faded memory. The balance between order and chaos is delicate, and entropy seems to always be lurking around the corner.

What may seem to be wild cohabitation to the uninitiated onlooker is actually a home that's evolved past the need for perfection; one that revolves around creative living and growing. Relics of experiences and projects fill every corner: That pile of wooden safari animals symbolizes a dangerous adventure, and the books tossed on the disheveled bed are remnants of a reading party.

Stanford University's d.school founder David Kelley maintains that when a space is considered an instrument for openness and originality, it becomes "a valuable tool that can help you create deep and meaningful collaborations." Guided by little minds that are more interested in new ideas than in keeping their feet off the furniture, child-filled houses embody what numerous academic studies and books such as *Simplicity Parenting* and *The Third Teacher* have supported: that an intentional environment can liberate individuality and potential. The realities of running a child-filled home confirm there are more important things to do than worry about fastidious order.

Savvy parents all over the world demonstrate the art of filling a home with dynamic childishness while refining its style. They have the ability to skillfully integrate the worlds of children and adults, which is the aesthetic equivalent of calmly cradling a baby in one hand and a cappuccino in the other: Picture books in a Paris apartment mingle with the uniformity of orange Penguin novels; a rope swing hangs over a Tunisian rug in a Brooklyn living room; and concrete halls in a house in Auckland become tricycle runways. It might come at the cost of stains, spills and fiascos, but homes like these have encouraged an intricate pattern of living that wards off potential stagnation.

Homes with children seem to reflect a psychological redesign of the parents that dwell in them more than any shift in style or pattern of living: Where there was once constant order or perhaps a little architectural egocentricity, there is now spontaneity and blissful altruism. The family dwelling might appear primal at times, but nothing is more civilized than humans expanding their capacities and reflecting these evolutions in the ways they live together.

TOK

& HIROMI

KISE

After founding TRUCK furniture nearly two decades ago, Tok and Hiromi Kise dreamed of creating an integrated space that combined their home, workshop and storefront into a single property. Thirteen years later, they made the move to a site in Osaka's Asahi ward that does all that and more: It accommodates their workshop, the store that sells their furniture, Hiromi's handmade leather goods shop called Atelier Shirokumasha, Bird Coffee (a café they opened so customers could relax with an espresso while shopping) and the house they live in with their young daughter, Hina. "We'd previously rented an array of separate buildings that were rather spread out from each other, so we wanted to gather them together into one cohesive connected unit," Tok says. After living in somewhat cramped quarters above their workshop in the Tamatsukuri neighborhood, it was a relief to relocate to an area where their family could live comfortably. Having these spaces in such close proximity allows Tok and Hiromi to transition between them with relative ease several times a day. "I give our cats and dogs breakfast first thing in the morning and then wander out into our beautiful garden to feed the birds," Tok says. "I spend the rest of my day going back and forth between the store, the workshop and Bird Coffee. I don't particularly separate work and rest, but it works for me." As Tok and Hiromi's busy schedules leave little time for cooking in the middle of the day, they often drop by Bird Coffee for a quick bite to eat and to catch up with each other over lunch. Tok enjoys spending his evenings relaxing with a beer or playing with the family's pets: Most of their five dogs and eight cats were adopted. "We kept finding newborn kittens just lying on the side of the street and ended up taking most of them in, so thankfully none of us have any allergies," he says, laughing. Constructing this property was a labor of love that the pair feels was entirely worthwhile: They've even published a book titled *TRUCK Nest* that documented their quest to create a place of their own. "The book is a record of the hard work, dedication and inspiration we put into envisioning this space," Tok says. "We longed for a space like this, and we made it a reality."

Above Right: Tok and Hiromi enjoy relaxing in their outdoor patio area over coffee in the morning or a glass of wine after work.

Following Page: Tok's friend and textile designer Akiko Takahashi made these sitting figurines out of clay and fabric. The boots on the left are from the Australian brand Rossi Boots and are Tok's favorite pair of shoes.

JENNI KAYNE

& RICHARD

EHRLICH

Growing up on the beaches of Santa Monica as a quintessential Southern California girl, Jenni Kayne learned to appreciate the qualities that a lucky and happy life in Los Angeles center around: light, play and comfort. She and her husband, real estate agent Richard Ehrlich, bought their home 10 years ago and made major moves to strip the property of its cold features. "I wanted to build a modern house that was all at once warm and functional," she says. Their success is reflected in many areas of the home, beginning with the entryway that was remodeled to incorporate large glass windows and high ceilings constructed with reclaimed Amish barn wood. "I really wanted the home to have a flow from the inside out," Jenni says. "The entry is where this starts." The expansion of energy from the front to the back of their house creates a sense of openness and lots of light. When the doors are open, there's a seamless connection between the outdoors and in, both visually and physically. "Anyone who knows me knows I love to entertain," Jenni says. "So being able to open all the doors to create an open space is one of my favorite parts of our home. I love that my kids are able to run from the backyard right into

the kitchen." Making a comfortable, playful home for their children, Tanner and Ripley, was key for the couple. They began renovating the house when Jenni was pregnant with Tanner six years ago, which allowed them to design with children in mind from the start. "We all hang out in the playroom—it's an easy, comfortable space," Jenni says. Practicality and relaxation are clear themes throughout the home, with Jenni describing her decorating style as "clean and minimal, but functional." Although her self-titled collection has a classic aesthetic, she's still often surrounded by patterns and colors as part of her daily creative process. She therefore keeps her home's palette neutral and chooses interesting objects and textures to draw the eye toward subtler details. "No one item jumps out at you, but I love to mix materials," Jenni says. "I have ceramics from Dora De Larios and Heather Levine, metals from Alma Allen and glass from Caleb Siemon." Despite their collection of decorative pieces, Jenni says that nothing inside their home is too precious or off-limits to her children, which helps reinforce the relaxed nature that defines both their family life and the home's atmosphere.

Left: The staircase is one of Jenni's favorite features of the home. She loves its shape, the curve of the railing and the natural light that floods in from the skylight.

Following Pages: The burlap light fixture is from Tim Clarke's shop in Santa Monica. The dining table is a Live Edge table from Lawson-Fenning and the chairs are vintage leather and metal pieces from Emmerson Troop.

Previous Page: These cherished sketches are a series of charcoal drawings from the 1960s that belonged to Jenni's father and have followed her every time she's moved. The African baskets were a gift from her mother.

Above Left: Jenni loves collecting ceramics for the earthiness and warmth they bring to a room. Her kitchen shelf contains ceramics by Victoria Morris Pottery, Alma Allen for Heath Ceramics, Humble Ceramics and Irving Place Studio.

HANNAH FERRARA

& MALCOLM

SMITLEY

Hannah Ferrara and Malcolm Smitley's home life is rooted in their love of entertaining. The couple moved to Portland, Oregon, from Asheville, North Carolina, in 2013 and made it a priority to find a house that could accommodate frequent gatherings with their family and friends. "Having a dining room large enough to fit a big table and a functioning kitchen spacious enough to prepare meals was key," says Hannah, the designer behind jewelry line Another Feather. Malcolm is a former chef who relishes using different cooking techniques to create an assortment of dishes for their guests. "Malcolm loves cooking over wood fires, so large meals with friends often include some sort of whole fish, roasted vegetables, a cheese plate and a large salad with fresh figs from our tree outside," Hannah says. As she and Malcolm both wanted a creative space at home, it was imperative that their house contain a suitable studio area with large windows to let in lots of natural light. They found the ideal spot in their attic workspace, which is outfitted with separate workstations, a central shared table and narrow desks that line the length of the walls. "After spending years with separate work schedules, we especially appreciate the fact that we now have the chance to both live and work together," Hannah says. They separate their work and home lives by limiting themselves to the studio during most of

the workday. This makes them feel more productive and mentally checked-in with their tasks. They also try to set aside at least one full day a week to take their minds off work and spend time outdoors. Hannah and Malcolm chose to balance out their home's rustic character by introducing modern pieces of furniture and are also discerning about what they surround themselves with. "I'm often visually drawn to so many things and want to bring them all home for inspiration, but I've found it hard to create or reflect if there isn't any blank space for me to think and rest my mind," she says. "If I do bring things in, I try and get rid of something in exchange." While Hannah and Malcolm miss their families on the East Coast, their efforts to foster community have helped them adjust to the rhythms of living in the Pacific Northwest. "People can live somewhere their whole lives without truly feeling at home, and then stay somewhere for a week and feel it right away," she says. "The West Coast is filled with components we didn't even realize we were lacking until we moved here, and I'm thankful for the chance to experience this definition of home."

In the following essay on page 148, we explore how entertaining at home can bring warmth to both your community and your kitchen.

Above: Hannah and Malcolm's coffee table is by Muuto and her favorite item in the room is a self-watering ceramic planter by Light + Ladder, which is great for keeping their ficus tree alive when they're traveling.

Following Pages: The couple loves hosting big brunches. The spread often served up at their gatherings includes pancakes, baked grapefruits, frittatas and fresh juice—as well as eggs Benedict, if they're feeling fancy.

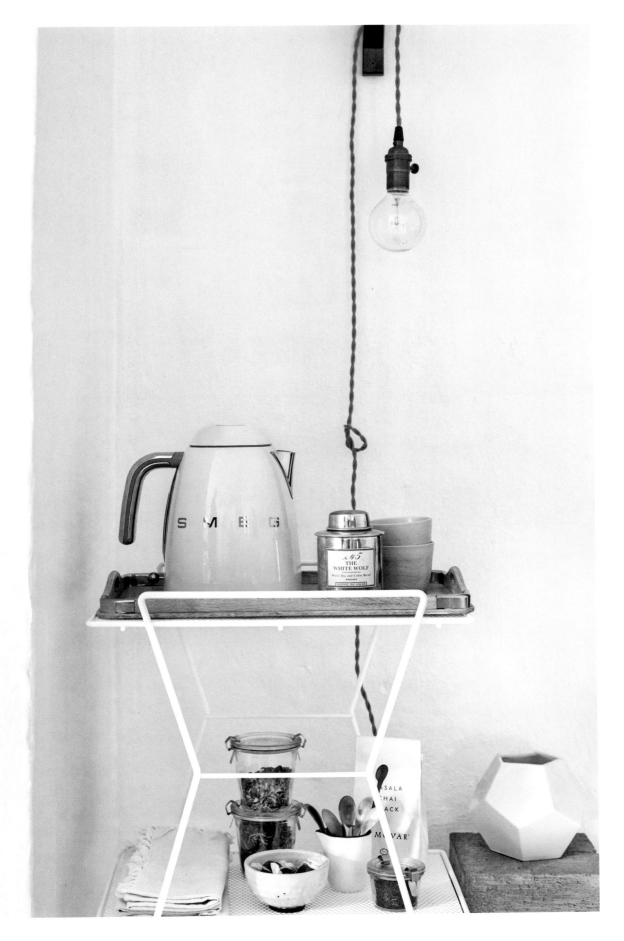

Above: Hannah keeps a linen pinboard in her studio with a rotating collection of clippings, images, textures and objects that help inspire her creative direction. Shapes, architecture and the human form also influence her work.

Right: Hannah and Malcolm love the soft light and slanted walls of their attic studio.

WORDS : JULIE POINTER

A SPACE
TO GATHER

Once viewed as a time-consuming and showy affair, modern home entertaining has now taken a more casual approach. By shifting our focus away from the superficial details, we can concentrate on the most important aspects of the meal: the people gathered around the table.

In a bygone time, home entertaining wasn't for the faint of heart. Having company once necessitated matching china, polished cutlery and plenty of chairs to go around. Messes were hidden from view and decadent roasts came out of massive French ovens—steaming, juicy and perfectly laden with lemon and thyme. For some, the thought of throwing a soiree can be daunting, partly because of the *Downton Abbey*-esque expectations that come with having a memorable dinner party.

Thankfully, our perspectives on hospitality have shifted from this archaic vision, and the idea of gathering together now means something more than just facilitating a grand performance. Inviting both friends and strangers into our homes has become an intimate act that welcomes participation—not only in the communal preparation of food but also in the messiness of daily life. (Truly, who has time to wipe down dusty baseboards or clean the expired jars out of the fridge?)

This more casual approach to hospitality no longer requires the host to forego days of eating just to finance the purchase of enough lobster tails to go around. And for those who subsist mostly on cereal for dinner, there's still hope for throwing a wildly successful fete without people going home hungry. No matter where your skills lie on the kitchen spectrum, there are myriad solutions for filling your house with friends (and filling their bellies, too).

The joy of gathering is found in the act of simply being together instead of the theater of putting on a good show. It doesn't matter whether meals are shared at a proper table, balanced on laps while sitting on the front porch or eaten while reclining in the middle of your studio—unconventional settings can leave us with more intriguing memories. Likewise, for those less adept at cooking, there's no shame in picking up pizza, sushi platters or Thai takeout, or asking pals to combine forces for a potluck.

Regardless of what's on the menu, the most important gesture is simply taking the initiative to gather folks together in the same place and time. Relationships deepen when we transcend the safe zone of meeting friends at restaurants, bars or the park. We invite them into the particulars and peculiarities of our homes, which are often mirrors of ourselves. The home compels a more candid exchange than other settings, if only because the frame with our mother's likeness in it or the heirloom on the mantel prompts a dialogue that otherwise would have never taken place.

By shifting our attitudes about the true motivation for dining together from grandeur to gathering, we can overcome our hosting fears to find that entertaining is an easily gained source of joy rather than a cumbersome task. It doesn't matter what you're eating or how the dishes are being served: There's no better way to spend your time, foster community and share your true self with the people you know and love than welcoming them (and their trays of treats) into your own comfortable abode.

HOMES FOR SIMPLICITY

Achieving simplicity in a home is less about relinquishing and more about refining. The residents in the following homes all embrace their personal values and have made their homes the physical manifestation of their beliefs. By keeping their spaces free of the nonessentials, they've made more room and time for what matters most to them. For some this might mean treating their homes as a canvas with blank walls that allow the mind to fill the gaps. Others may prefer to be surrounded by curious sentimental objects that are imbued with memories of loved ones. Sometimes a clutter-clearing renovation is required to get back to basics, though some homeowners may prefer to start from scratch to build a new structure that reflects their values. Although the criteria for these simple spaces may vary from minimal to eclectic and large to small, each living environment prioritizes its dwellers' take on what is considered essential.

JONAS

& CHRISTINE

BJERRE-POULSEN

On a typical morning in Vedbæk, which was once a small fishing village, Jonas and Christine Bjerre-Poulsen spend breakfast with their family watching the fishermen steer into port with their freshest catches. The historic home they live in with their kids, Benjamin and Clara, overlooks the harbor in this suburb of northern Copenhagen and is surrounded by an idyllic wooded landscape. "Since I work in central Copenhagen and get the buzz of the city every day, Vedbæk is the perfect place to come home to after a long day," Jonas says. The Bjerre-Poulsens' house was built in 1911 by architects H. Wright and E.V. Marston during a period when many coastal villas were being constructed along the shores. "At that time, architecture from southern Germany and northern Italy was very much in vogue, so it was built in a Tyrolean style with a very high roofline and wooden balconies that overlooked the sea," Jonas says. Despite the architects' original intentions, many different previous owners had contributed haphazard renovations to the house that had resulted in seven different types of mismatched flooring, add-ons and conflicting styles. Drawing on his work as an architect and designer for his company, Norm.Architects, Jonas worked to unearth the home's old-world charm by deconstructing the interior, redecorating the rooms in one cohesive

style and keeping the most charming original details. "It made the house feel much more unified inside and really focused on the beautiful original decor," he says. They left some old details to contrast with the new, such as repurposing the original herringbone flooring to make their kitchen counter. Although the result is decidedly minimalist, the family fills these wide-open spaces with indoor skateboarding and large parties. "We really believe you should use a house and everything in it, so we use it hard for playing," Jonas says, laughing. "Of course the house gets worn, but some elements become more interesting as they age." The neighborhood outside Jonas and Christine's domestic playground also lends itself to a laid-back lifestyle: After living in the area for several years, they've found themselves settling into the cozy suburb's pace with regular walks on the pier, picnics on the beach and ice cream on the marina after dinner in the summer months. "Home isn't only about the space you live in, but also the area," Jonas says. "It's about a sense of belonging to a certain place."

In the following interview on page 164, Jonas discusses his personal views on minimalism and tells us about his work as a designer and architect.

Previous Pages: The light fixtures that hang in Jonas and Christine's kitchen are by the Danish brand Frama. Menu, Danish designer Tobias Tøstesen and Jonas's design firm, Norm.Architects, created the assorted cutting boards.

Above: Jonas took the photographs on the wall—they're of the area around their home, a nightscape from the beach, their kids in a hammock and an image from their wedding day. The images hang over a pair of daybeds that Jonas adapted from bunk beds as the kids got older.

Left: Jonas often works from home with the kids playing around him—he finds it easier to concentrate with a fair amount of noise. The main light fixture is by Danish architect Grethe Meyer.

Above Right: Jonas' team at Norm.Architects created all of the objects on the mantel—the clock is made out of Carrara marble from Italy.

INTERVIEW : AMY WOODROFFE

BACK
TO BASICS

For designer and architect Jonas Bjerre-Poulsen, the Danish minimalist
style that defines his work is also an important part of his home. He speaks
about his extensive renovation process and explains why our living spaces
should be in a constant state of flux.

Please tell us about the process of stripping your house back to the basics. — I'm very minimalist in my taste and have always preferred modernist houses, but when we saw this historic house, there was just something about it that resonated. The Mediterranean elements were very overdone by the previous owner, though, so we had to remove a lot of the interior— it seemed like a theatrical backdrop from a movie set in Tuscany! During the renovations, we were careful to keep the most beautiful original details and ornaments. The house also had seven floor types in different layers, so we leveled them and cast a new magnetite floor as an industrial contrast to the ornate walls and ceilings. I'd seen this kind of contrast before in art galleries and museums, and I love how keeping everything very simple and clean really amplifies the historic details.

What's your philosophy on material possessions in the home? — Our home is a microcosm where everything has to balance. If I bring a new chair into the home, everything might suddenly need to move around in order to regain the balance. Material possessions are all about tactility, simplicity and timelessness. When we were younger, we sometimes bought more fashionable or poor-quality items, but you quickly learn that this doesn't make sense in the long run. The joy of those fast-fashion items is very limited. Now we try to find things that are really simple in their expression, work well, are durable and that we can keep on looking at forever and ever.

How does a little wear and tear add character to a pristine home? — We use our house for playing, partying and having fun. Some elements become more beautiful with the patina of use, but other elements don't age so well, like the white walls. Once in a while, a lamp gets knocked over if I'm playing soccer with my son, Benjamin, in the living room or if the kids are doing Parkour on the furnishings. But that's just what happens in our family home.

Do you believe that a home can ever be "finished"? — No, I don't believe that anything is static—everything changes all the time. Some people have the idea of a home being finite, and those people take comfort in the ability to control the small universe of a home. But I really like to treat my home in the opposite way by sometimes removing everything from a room and starting over. Changing the position of things can give them new life. Objects tend to grow into a certain position in the home otherwise, and after a while they go by almost unnoticed. It's a good thing to stir things up and not finish them: For us, owning an old house means there's always something to do, and by the time we're "finished," we could easily start all over again.

What advice do you have for people who aspire to live more minimally without losing the warmth in their home? — It's important that the few things you have and the space you live in work really well in terms of natural daylight, natural materials and natural beauty. I've seen so many minimalist spaces that feel cold and unwelcoming because they're made entirely from hard, industrial or artificial materials. If you use natural elements in the right way, a minimal space can feel warm and welcoming even though it's sparse. That's one reason why we've used mostly natural colors and materials in our home.

What is the essence of home? — I believe a home needs to be a sanctuary, a place where I can totally relax, unwind and forget about what's outside. Sometimes it's a place for work, but more importantly, it's a place for being together with family and friends.

MIQUEL ALZUETA

& ÁFRICA POSSE

Before becoming an art collector and gallerist, Miquel Alzueta spent time wandering the streets of Paris, often finding himself drawn into small antique shops. During that time, he first encountered the works of influential French designers Jean Prouvé and Charlotte Perriand, and something clicked. This introduction soon turned into a deep obsession and the 1950s style of functional furnishings permeated every aspect of his life. "One doesn't choose his whims, his passions or his follies," Miquel says. "I got there by being curious, and I turned it into a way of learning, a way of living and, later on, into a job and a business." He started looking for Prouvé and Perriand's pieces, buying them and offering them to customers. "Each acquisition meant a period of trouble for my finances, but I loved to collect them," he says. Miquel was rewarded for his risky decisions with a collection that grew into the foundation of his personal home near Barcelona's city center, where he now lives with his wife, África Posse, and her son, Santiago. The building is located in a small suburb at the foot of Mt. Tibidabo called Pedralbes

(Catalan for "white stones"), which is known for its architectural history and for having some of the most well-preserved Gothic architecture in western Europe. Miquel was originally drawn to their building because it spoke to his passion for French design. "Catalan culture has been greatly influenced by French culture, but this wasn't often reflected on an architectural level. This building does have this influence, though, and I like that," Miquel says. The structure was designed in the 1940s by Raimon Duran i Reynals, who respected French and neoclassical styles. With África's background in antique dealing and Miquel's passion for art, they've filled their home with pieces from their well-developed personal collections, which are directly connected to their personal values. Miquel appreciates how these accumulated items add to the ongoing history of a household. "If the home is old, it speaks of tradition and the past. If it's new, it talks about us," he says. "Beyond the beauty and utility is a sign of identity that speaks of the way we understand the world."

Previous Page: This wooden chair was designed by Kenzō Tange, a Japanese architect who was greatly influenced by the Rationalism design movement.

Above: The artwork in Miquel and África's kitchen was painted by Miquel Mont, the light fixture is a Serge Mouille creation and the chairs were designed by Charlotte Perriand.

Left: The shelves on the back wall were made by Charlotte Perriand and the chairs are from Prouvé, Perriand and Mathieu Matégot. The large black painting is by Imi Knoebel.

JESSE KAMM

& LUKE BROWER

Jesse Kamm and Luke Brower love the neighborhood they live in for the community pride and their friendly, helpful neighbors. "Mount Washington is a strange and wonderful hippie hideaway with beautiful architecture, breathtaking mountains, nature reserves and views to die for," says Jesse, a fashion designer. "I never thought I could raise a child in Los Angeles until I found this place." Although they adore their California house, they spend most of the summer months living in their second home in Isla Carenero, Panama. "Living in Panama brings us closer to nature and makes us so aware of our consumption," Jesse says. "We wanted to bring that ethos of sustainable living back to our life in Los Angeles." Jesse and Luke began by outfitting the L.A. home they share with their son, Julien, with a recycling device that directs gray water out to the yard for landscape watering, an efficient water-heating system and a flat roof that will accommodate the photovoltaic solar panel unit they plan on installing soon. The house was built in 1949 and originally functioned as a mountain retreat; its interior feels like a mid-century lodge, but its location on a hill among a canopy of palm and conifer trees reminds them of their house in Panama. "The way it opens up onto the decks and patios gives a real sense of indoor-outdoor living, which is perfect for the weather in California," Jesse says. "We love the

way the living room, dining room, music nook and kitchen all feel like one space but are separate and distinct at the same time." Although Jesse and Luke left most of the house untouched, they adapted it by building new pinewood doors, painting the walls white and converting one of the bedrooms into a studio for Jesse to work on her clothing designs. She's operated out of a combined live-work space for more than 10 years now, but it still takes lots of practice and a strong will to separate the two. "I make a real effort to shut down the computers, turn off my phone and close the studio doors when I decide I'm done working for the day," she says. The minimalist aesthetic that characterizes her self-titled label is also reflected in her lifestyle choices, from her essentialist philosophy on interior decorating to her keen awareness of her family's consumption habits. "I came from a home where I learned about creating beauty from very little, as my parents' house was simple, efficient and geared toward practicality," Jesse says. "Anytime I have the instinct to get 'tricky,' whether it's with my collection or a design choice in our house, I think long and hard about what value it really adds."

In the following essay on page 186, Jesse talks in greater depth about her philosophy on sustainable living.

Above: Luke's father and Jesse's mother each designed one of the bowls on the bench in the background.

Above Right: Julien loves surfing, hiking with his parents and playing with Jesse's old Lego bricks, which he transforms into all sorts of amazing vehicles and dwellings. He has quite an imagination, and Jesse and Luke enjoy going along for the ride.

Left: Luke and Jesse built the daybed in this room. Her vintage drafting lamp reminds her of her father's drafting table.

Above: Some of Jesse's favorite books are *New Fashion Japan* by Leonard Koren, *Irving Penn Regards the Work of Issey Miyake* by Irving Penn and *Georgia O'Keeffe and the Camera: The Art of Identity* by Susan Danly.

Following Page: The family loves to go surfing together. Their wet suits were designed by Vissla and Xcel and the camp stools are from Kalon Studios and Nico Nico's Wilderness Collection.

WORDS : JESSE KAMM

FOREST FOR
THE TREES

Spending time in Panama's rainforest has given Jesse Kamm a unique perspective on sustainable living. She talks about the eco-conscious features of her homes and offers some insight on how to make our spaces more environmentally friendly.

Living more simply and consuming less just takes awareness. Some of us have become so accustomed to living a lavish lifestyle: I'm not talking about wearing Hermès and diamonds, but things like getting fuel from a pump, having water and power delivered directly to our homes and being able to obtain food with a simple swipe of our credit cards. These luxuries can be wonderful, but they separate us from the reality of what we're using and how our actions affect the earth. Over the years I've made it a point to check in and remember that I'm a part of my environment, not apart from it. This has led me to making better choices in my effort to live a sustainable lifestyle.

My husband, Luke, and I designed our house in Panama from scratch to be as sustainable as possible. There are no direct water, sewer or power lines available near our home, and running water and electricity are essential to living comfortably in the jungle. So we simply set out to use the best available technology we could find while remaining eco-conscious: We store rainwater in a 1,250-gallon tank, the sun powers all our energy needs and our waste is turned into compost that goes into the garden to nourish our plants. Our home is a quarter-mile walk from the boat dock and another five-minute boat ride into town, so every single bit of food, piece of wood, bottle of sunscreen or tank of propane we need must be carried across the island on foot through the humid and muddy rainforest. All of these circumstances make us a highly responsible and effective family when it comes to our consumption habits. We purchase only what we need, and we make darn sure we don't waste a drop of our resources. We spend time in Panama in order to connect with the earth—the feeling my family gets from living off nature's bounty is unbeatable.

Most of the living space in our Panama house is outside. We spend a lot of time on our giant wraparound porch that sits up in the jungle canopy—swinging in hammocks, drinking coffee and listening to the birds. We've managed to build a home that harnesses what nature provides and uses the space we have efficiently. I love that I watched and helped as my husband drove every nail into the structure as it came together plank by plank. I feel like I know every inch of this home.

If something goes wrong in the house, we know how to repair it. It's the ultimate example of simple and efficient living.

Anyone can live more efficiently by being mindful of the resources they're using. The first step in making a more sustainable home is living a more sustainable lifestyle. Little things like taking shorter showers, setting the thermostat to a reasonable temperature, washing only full loads of laundry and turning off the lights make a huge difference. When you do have to replace things, choose something that's as efficient as possible, such as LED lightbulbs. If you're in the northern hemisphere, make sure you have lots of south-facing, double-paned windows as they let in and retain solar radiation. If you live in a cold climate, spray-foam insulation works well for sealing all those little air leaks. If you live where it's warm, design your space with cross-breeze ventilation and shade in mind. Planting deciduous trees will keep your home cool in the summer and warm during the winter months—nature is your accomplice! We also have an organic container garden, which in no way feeds our family completely but does teach our son where food comes from.

Solar-power systems are amazing but need to be thoughtfully designed. Start with solar hot-water panels, as they get you a lot more bang for your buck then photovoltaic cells (which can be tackled once your needs for hot water are fulfilled). Water conservation is a huge issue, so plumbing your house so that gray water from your sink and shower flows out into the garden via drip lines is a great technique for saving water. Collecting rainwater is quite easy as well—if you plan on using the water for irrigation, hook your gutters up to a cistern and voilà!

People sometimes seem confused about what it means to go green. It doesn't mean rushing out and buying a bunch of new stuff while you throw out your perfectly good stuff. That just leads to the production of more things, which is the opposite of sustainable. Sustainability means choosing quality items, caring for them well and keeping them for as long as possible. It means consuming less—fewer clothes, gadgets, new cars and processed foods. Most of the time, living more sustainably only enhances our lifestyle and rarely inhibits it. It gives us a lot of pride and keeps us closely connected to our surroundings.

JACK DAHL

& KRISTOFFER

SAKURAI

Copenhagen's Frederiksstaden district is home to many of the city's most archetypal sights, including picturesque alleys, seaside parks and the home of the royal family. Art director Jack Dahl and Kristoffer Sakurai, who manages Valentino Copenhagen, chose to build their life in this neighborhood because of its accessibility to the vibrant local culture—and the 18th-century home they found that sits at the center of it. "We love it here: It feels like living in Copenhagen, London, Moscow and Paris all at the same time," Jack says. With an abundance of activity outside their front door, the couple designed the interior of their apartment to reflect a quieter and humbler pace of life. Jack is the founder of Homework, a studio specializing in brand expression and communication, and the duo found inspiration in the company's manifesto: "Simplifying so the essential can shine." They rely mostly on shades of gray and simple sleek lines to achieve this aesthetic, "But we always add a personal twist, or a little je ne sais quoi," Jack says. Simplicity became the foundation for the renovation, and from there they removed some of the walls to give it a more modern, spacious feel and used minimalist decor to make elegant shapes. The light that filters in through the windows creates a shifting backdrop throughout the day and is one of their favorite natural features because it gives the apartment depth without having to add overpowering furnishings. Jack and Kristoffer have added a few personal pieces and idiosyncratic details to the unembellished space, including the large collection of artwork and books they keep around for visual nourishment. "They constantly tempt us with procrastination, adventure, inspiration, admiration and desire," Kristoffer says. They both read a lot: Kristoffer enjoys historical literature, whereas Jack is more into art, fashion and interior-design books, as well as monographs and magazines. Aside from the couple's library, their most prized possession is without a doubt their dog, Jackson: Since adopting the pup, the couple has experienced an even greater influx of love and comfort within their home. "It's family," Jack says.

Previous Page: Kristoffer loves historical literature and always has a number of books on his bedside table. Jack keeps notes, scented candles, sketchbooks and his iPad on his side.

Above: Jack and Kristoffer's dog, Jackson, isn't technically allowed on their Antonio Citterio sofa, but he has yet to take no for an answer. The black-and-white geometric rug is from IKEA.

Left: The couple is partial to small coffee tables.
The gray marble table is from e15, the classic
black stone table is from Poul Kjærholm and
the silver table is by HAY. The artwork in the
background is from the Nils Stærk gallery in
Copenhagen.

JONATHAN

& ANNABEL

TUCKEY

"I love our house because of what it once was and what it has become," architectural designer Jonathan Tuckey says about the 19th-century steel fabricators' workshop that he renovated with his wife, Annabel. The potential of taking a derelict space and turning it into something special had major appeal to the couple, who live in North Kensington with their two teenage daughters, Tasmina and Thea, and their dog, Tarka. Known as the "Collage House" in design circles, the large L-shaped space has been adapted to accommodate the needs of their growing family. Over the renovation process, they enjoyed discovering what was necessary to "domesticate" an existing industrial building while keeping enough of the original to ground the new home in its context. "This approach was chosen to encourage a patina of use and to collaborate with the existing building in spirit and texture," Jonathan says. "Over the past 10 years as our family has grown in the space, the materials have accumulated the marks of life, gatherings, celebrations and birthdays. Modernizing heritage design means taking a continuum into consideration." For the initial renovation, Jonathan and Annabel stripped the building bare, including the partitions and asbestos-filled roofs, and used it as a studio before redesigning it to address their personal needs for a home. "During that time, it was used for exhibitions, parties and photo shoots to see how the space worked and felt," Jonathan says. He and Annabel found the structure's historic features appealing, so they kept some of these ordinary aspects, such as the writing on the walls, the paintwork on the bricks and the original signage. These features blend together with the modern decor and suit the building's overall structure. "The existing building is brick and timber, and we complemented it with new brick, pigmented concrete, Douglas fir and both larch and beech plywood," he says. They also added elements for their daughters: Tasmina and Thea shared a room downstairs for their first five years, but as they've grown older they've moved to their own spaces with a pivoting wall in between that allows the girls' rooms to become one if necessary. "We appreciate that we can adapt the space as they continue to grow up," Jonathan says.

Left: Some of Jonathan's favorite kitchen tools are Le Creuset cast-iron pots, a Bialetti coffeepot, a collection of old wooden kitchen boards and some 1970s Danish melamine items. The artwork in the background is a photograph by Richard Avedon for *Vogue*.

Above Left: The family created the garden from scratch: They grow more than 40 different herbs and a variety of produce, including olives, pears, apples, figs and plums.

Above Right: Jonathan's mother, Louise Tuckey, designed the
rug in this room. Jonathan found the chair at an antique fair in
Ardingly, Sussex.

Following Page: Jonathan and Annabel bought this armchair
on Golborne Road and had it reupholstered by Pat Giddens,
and the stool was found at a market in Harare, Zimbabwe.

DAN HONEY

& PAUL MARCUS

FUOG

Dan Honey and Paul Marcus Fuog seem to have cracked the code to making the most efficient use of a small home. They live with their young daughter, Eike, in an apartment designed by architect Clare Cousins in one of Melbourne's bustling laneways. "Although we both work in design, we felt really strongly about getting Clare involved," Dan says. "She has an unfussy but warm approach and understood the space and how to occupy it in a way we didn't." Dan and Paul, who are both entrepreneurs, collaborated with Clare to incorporate elements of Japanese, modern Californian and Scandinavian design into their home. "Our place is a strange mongrel of the three with a little bit of Australia thrown in," Dan says. Determined to maximize the amount of space in the small inner-city apartment, the pair sacrificed a sprawling private bedroom in favor of a more modest approach. "Our bed is now just a cozy sleeping nook that opens into the living room and is wonderfully connected to the rest of the house," Dan says. "It's become one of our favorite things about the apartment: Eike plays in it during the day, and I spend evenings lying there and chatting with Paul, who might be hanging out on the couch." They employed strategic design decisions to open up the apartment and create the illusion of space, including outfitting the house with large pull-out drawers under Eike's bed and in the dividing joinery between the couple's bedroom and living areas.

"A limited color and material palette is important to create a sense of space, openness and fluidity where one space seamlessly flows into another," Dan says. While living in such close quarters can make it difficult to separate business and leisure when working from home, they respect the importance of switching off and devoting time to each other. "We have a rule of no digital devices during the first hour of the morning and the last hour before bed," Dan says. "It helps us both feel more in control and allows us to enjoy the quiet." Mornings often begin with a wake-up call from Eike, who jumps into their bed with a rousing request for muesli. They then open the blinds—a symbolic gesture that happens only when they're ready to let in the day and the chaos of the city below. Dan and Paul travel a lot for work, but they've grown to appreciate the stability and solidity that comes with owning a home. "With travel comes transience," Dan says. "It's romantic and filled with wonder, but it can also feel unstable and unsafe at times. We feel very lucky to be able to experiment with how and where we live, but it's reassuring to know that if we go too far or if things get out of control, then we can always come back to our base."

In the following interview on page 214, we speak with Clare Cousins, Dan and Paul's architect, about her distinct design process for small spaces.

Left: Dan and Paul pass along most of their favorite books to friends, but a few titles they've kept and often return to are *The Shock of the New* by Robert Hughes, *Don't Take These Drawings Seriously* by Nathalie Du Pasquier and *A. Quincy Jones* by Cory Buckner.

Above Left: Their ceramic sink, which was designed by Villeroy & Boch, is a bit large for such a small home, but it doubles as a laundry sink and also used to be a bathtub when their daughter, Eike, was little.

Above: The artwork is by Nathalie Du Pasquier and the
Pigeon Light on the shelf was designed by Ed Carpenter.

Above Right: Dan and Paul bought this Eames chair because
of their appreciation for the brand's philosophy and approach
to blending work and life. It serves as a reminder that there's
no need to separate work from everyday life if you truly love
what you do.

ECONOMY
OF SPACE

Living in a small space doesn't mean you have to compromise on your quality of life. Clare Cousins, the architect who led Dan Honey and Paul Marcus Fuog's apartment renovation, offers advice on how to make the most efficient use of a smaller home.

What are the benefits of living in a smaller space? — Living smaller is more affordable as small spaces are more efficient to heat and use fewer materials to construct. They're also intimate and cozy when designed well, which brings a feeling of connectedness to the occupants.

What space-conscious architecture around the world do you find inspiring? — We're spoiled with space in Australia. Unfortunately, this has led to horizontal growth, where cities have low density and housing is spreading further away from amenities and public transportation. In Europe and Japan, cities are dense and apartment living or small housing is the norm. We've been inspired by various Japanese projects for their innovative occupation of modest space—the mix of traditional and modern architecture often creates spaces for multiple purposes, such as tatami rooms in Japan that act as a living room during the day and a sleeping space at night. The use of screens also encourages engagement when open and creates privacy when closed. We should consider how a space might have multiple functions: For example, can a living room be both a study and a guest bedroom at different times of the day? We should avoid having rooms that aren't used on a daily basis.

Designing small spaces must come with a lot of compromise. How do you help clients assess what's really essential? — "Quality over quantity" is generally what convinces clients to consider smaller spaces. They might consider that one functional bathroom is ample for a family of four and a parking space isn't necessary given their proximity to public transport. In our consumerist culture, having a smaller home makes you consider your purchases and place more importance on what you choose to live with.

Are there any common design elements and approaches you recommend for maximizing small spaces? — Think about how your current spaces are being used: Could they be used differently and for multiple purposes? Consider the flooring—a single material throughout a home feels more expansive than one with a different finish in each room. Smaller spaces benefit from a limited material palette as the surfaces flow from one to another. For Dan and Paul's apartment, we used a single material— plywood—as it could be used for the floor, walls and joinery. Plywood's visual warmth provides a neutral, hard-wearing backdrop for family life. Rationalize your furniture, as many loose items can make a space

feel smaller. Consolidate one large storage area for the bulk of your storage requirements, and use high-level storage, like the mezzanine over Dan and Paul's bathroom that stores surfboards and infrequently used items. Integrating and concealing appliances such as the refrigerator, dishwasher and washing machine visually streamlines a space, and built-in furniture uses space efficiently and reduces the amount of loose furniture.

What are some ways to get around the challenges presented by small homes, such as privacy and storage? — Living small requires flexibility and creativity. Large sliding doors enable spaces to be either private or open, which allows occupants to adapt the flow of the home to suit their needs. Smaller homes should also have access to ample natural light and ventilation to enhance the perception of space. Well-considered storage is critical, as clutter leads to small spaces feeling smaller. Not all storage spaces need to be concealed, though: Shelving can be both functional and decorative.

What are some of the positive effects that smaller residences can have on the wider community? — Smaller homes and higher-density living encourage engagement with open public spaces and parks, which promotes street life in the city. A critical mass of people allows for more efficiency and a better provision of services such as schools, public transportation and hospitals. Well-planned, higher-density living also allows for houses to be in closer proximity to work and activities, which helps reduce our reliance on cars and natural resources. Plus, people who live close to work are happier! Walking around your neighborhood promotes neighborly interactions and connections between people, and eyes on the street are good for neighborhood security.

How do small environments impact our relationship and interaction with outside spaces? — Living in a smaller home creates a greater sense of connection to our surroundings, whether it's a city or a landscape. A small log cabin would provide shelter and amenities yet encourage you to head outdoors to enjoy fresh air and nature. Similarly, a small urban home provides the necessary comforts inside while the city's gardens, parks and public spaces draw you outside. Being able to enjoy what's outside the home is just as important as what's enjoyed inside the home.

RIEKO

OHASHI

One of Rieko Ohashi's favorite things about living in Hayama—a small beachside town just south of Tokyo—is its proximity to nature. "I live by the water in the peaceful and picturesque countryside, and there are some beautiful mountains nearby," says Rieko, a designer at Fog Linen. "I was tired of living in Tokyo and moved to Hayama for a quieter lifestyle: It's a great place to design and create because you can really think deeply about your ideas." Rieko lives by herself in a traditional Japanese dwelling that was constructed about 80 years ago. Living alone gives her ample time and space to work at her own pace, often leaving various pieces of fabric spread out across several tables. Although she makes frequent trips to Tokyo for work, she's diligent about setting aside time for herself and finding moments of peace throughout the day. She also takes note of her days off and firmly sticks to them. "I like going for evening walks along the beach and make a point to relax at night with a long bath, a home-cooked meal and a glass of sake," she says. When decorating her home, she paid careful attention to creating a balanced color spectrum throughout the house, as well as using materials that complemented each other. "It's important for me to maintain a sense of balance in terms of color, quantity and layout, whether in my designs or in my home," she says. "I often make unexpected discoveries when I physically line up certain pieces alongside each other rather than letting them remain as abstract concepts in my head." Although her house is minimally furnished, some of her favorite items include her futon, bathtub and various pieces of Danish furniture. "I didn't expect them to work in a traditional Japanese house, but they've blended in rather nicely and add a lot to the overall mood," she says. "A home is the perfect reflection of its inhabitant: You don't have to look too hard to see a person's essence manifest itself in the interior." Rieko enjoys entertaining and frequently prepares fresh meals for her guests. Many of the ingredients she uses in her dishes come from her garden, where she grows a variety of produce including yuzu, kumquats, plums and *sansho* (Japanese peppers). "Different flowers bloom with the changing of the seasons, and I love coming home to the scent of the garden," Rieko says. "I like drinking my morning coffee and looking out the window to see what flowers have blossomed overnight—it really warms my heart." For Rieko, living in Hayama presents a welcome change from life in a bustling metropolis. "Home is a place where I can reset and recharge," she says. "No matter how late I have to work in Tokyo, I come back to my house in Hayama and immediately feel at ease."

In the following essay on page 224, we explore some of the enduring concepts in Japan's history of domestic rituals.

Left: The hallway that leads to the entrance passes through Rieko's workspace, which is where she keeps her sewing machine, fabrics, worktables and mannequins.

Above Right: Although Rieko works with an assortment of fabrics, her favorite material to work with is chambray. She's also a fan of herringbone and the Lithuanian hemp fabric that she uses to create many of Fog Linen's collections.

WORDS : DANIELLE DEMETRIOU

AN ANCIENT
APPROACH

A few of Japan's most revered domestic gurus—from 14th-century monks to modern-day interior-design aficionados—share some wise words on how to bring an element of Zen into our home environments.

The Japanese are celebrated for their talents in many art forms, yet the art of Japanese homemaking doesn't seem to garner the same level of appreciation as others. There's an intrinsic serenity, cleanliness and functionality to many Japanese homes: the neat alignment of shoes in the *genkan* (the home's entryway), the discretion of sliding screens in *ryokan* (the homely inns), the quietness of minimalist decor—these signature details are all elemental in achieving this art.

The foundations of Japanese home rituals are rooted in the centuries-old ruminations of spiritually (and domestically) enlightened monks, tea masters, warriors and philosophers. Today this innate domestic wisdom lives on in the nation's modern-day homeowners, who prepare intricate bento-box lunches (complete with panda faces made of seaweed) before sunrise and craft flower arrangements that reflect the passing of the seasons.

But what is the essence of these harmonious households, and how can dwellings elsewhere achieve the same kind of Zen? The answer seems to lie in a precise mix of keeping things simple, clean and tidy, with a hint of nature thrown in for good measure.

Here, a few of Japan's celebrated domestic gurus offer some advice.

The Minimal Home
Masaharu Anesaki's seminal 1930s work, *Art, Life and Nature in Japan*, delves into the *wabi-sabi* concept of simple imperfect beauty in the home and highlights the way that minimal items and a sense of open space can create a deeper serenity than a room crammed full of objects. "The Japanese room then, though to the Western eye bare and devoid of artistic decoration, is nevertheless the product of a refined artistic sense and a place of sincere aesthetic enjoyment or serene meditation," he wrote.

The Flower-filled Home
Flowers go hand in hand with traditional Japanese residences, from asymmetrical ikebana displays in the *tokonoma* alcove (a sacred space showcasing items of appreciation) to garden blooms arranged on the kitchen table. But they're not there simply because they're pretty: Their presence taps into a deeper Japanese consciousness of the harmony between man, nature and the infinite cycle of life. As Sōfu Teshigahara, the founder of the early 20th-century Sōgetsu School of Ikebana, once said: "Ikebana will fail if its ultimate goal is the imitation of nature, even if the imitation is more or less perfect. One cannot just take a piece of it and try to re-create it—one takes a piece of nature and adds something that was not there."

The Unfussy Home
Yoshida Kenkō, the 14th-century monk who penned Japan's medieval masterwork *Essays in Idleness* (*Tsurezuregusa*), believed that simple antiques, a penchant for tidiness and a lovingly overgrown garden can help create the perfect domestic abode: "The man is to be envied who lives in a house, not of the modern, garish kind, but set among venerable trees, with a garden where plants grow wild and yet seem to have been disposed with care, verandas and fences tastefully arranged, and all its furnishings simple but antique," he wrote.

The Clean Home
Masako Ito, a popular young stylist and homemaking guru, encourages people to rid their homes of *moyari*, which she interprets as "unwanted air." Masako suggests paying careful attention to areas that are prone to creating moyari by regularly cleaning the space underneath a chair, the base of a toothbrush holder and even the back of the fridge's vegetable tray. "Basically, the air is in the places you don't really look at or ignore," she explains. These areas should also ideally be cleaned using a *zokin* cloth made from old T-shirts to avoid disrupting the domestic harmony of a home.

The Tidy Home
Marie Kondo became famous with her best-selling book *The Life-Changing Magic of Tidying Up: The Japanese Art of Decluttering and Organizing*. The gist of her "KonMari Method" is simple: Get rid of anything that doesn't spark joy in your life. The book is filled with tips from rolling up T-shirts like sushi to thanking unwanted items for their service before discarding them. The result could be a space as serene as a Shinto shrine.

TRINE

ANDERSEN

& MARTIN NEVE

The aesthetic of Trine Andersen's design company ferm LIVING was inspired by her grandmother's appreciation for skilled craftspeople who make quality goods with homemade characteristics. "When my grandmother said that someone was *ferm på fingrene* (skilled with their hands), it was high praise indeed," Trine says. When she and her husband, Martin Neve, who is the studio's art director, were house hunting, they searched for a place where lasting memories could be made with their children. They purchased space in a building that originally functioned as a pencil factory before going on to have many other lives—when they moved in, it was ending its time as a recording studio. "It was made up of 10 completely soundproof rooms with lowered ceilings and raised floors," Trine says. "The first thing we did was clear everything away: All the walls were torn down and the floors removed. " Inside this newfound openness, they installed a brand-new kitchen, ample living space and the main office for their growing company. But after using the space for both work and play for a few years, they eventually needed a change. "In the beginning, we had both our private home and the design studio in the apartment with only a door separating them," Trine says. When the studio became too small to fit both their employees and their children,

August and baby Saga, they decided to move the business to a larger area and turn the entire space into their home. Even though ferm LIVING's headquarters are now separated from the couple's home, the company's design ethos still continues to resonate throughout their apartment. "We look for the same things in what we create at work as we do for our private home," Trine says. Many of the company's products are found around the space: The bedding, marble coffee tables and plant pots were all born at ferm LIVING. Trine pulls inspiration for her furnishings from both her professional and personal life. "Everything inspires me," she says. "Everything I see and experience goes through a filter in my brain: Some of it's stored away, and when you put these stored impressions together, they might end up becoming a product or an idea." As for other additions, Trine and Martin carefully choose the objects that sit alongside their own designs. "We try to select only things that are unique, handcrafted or such good quality that we can keep them for a long time—things we don't get tired of looking at," she says.

In the following essay on page 236, we explore how large warehouse spaces can be transformed into personal creative abodes.

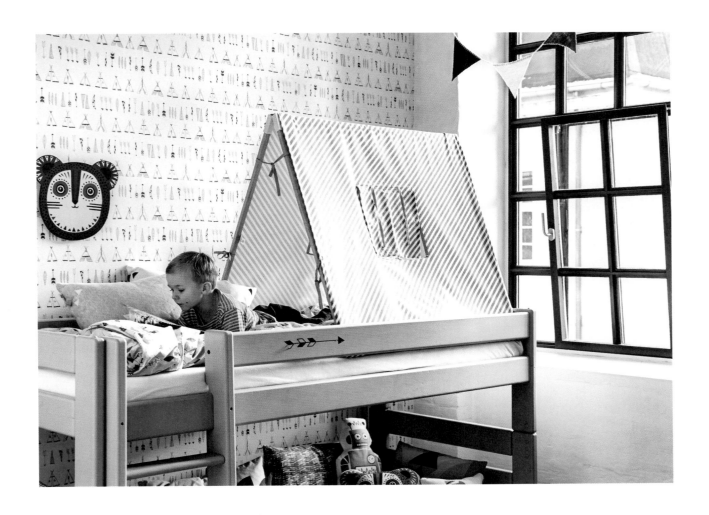

Left: Trine and Martin's daybed is by Skovshoved Møbelfabrik, the lounge chair is an Eames design and the light fixture is by Søren Rose. Danish artist Mie Olise created the large artwork on the wall.

Following Page: The wool sculptures on the bookshelf are made by Elkeland, and the bird next to them was a gift from a good friend. The hand sculptures were vintage finds and the vases were designed by ferm LIVING.

Eleanor Lambert: Still He

WORDS : SAM EICHBLATT

INDUSTRIAL
DOMESTICITY

Living in spaces that weren't originally meant for families has its benefits (like high ceilings) and drawbacks (like the lack of power outlets). But if we can manage to adapt these cavernous realms, they provide all the room in the world for personal growth.

Making a home inside a space that wasn't originally designed to contain the small and intimate rituals of daily life has always been associated with the creative classes. Domestic and industrial architecture stand at opposite ends of the spectrum: The former is orderly, private, scaled to suit human bodies and neatly finished, while the latter is improvisational at best with intricate webs of extension cords growing where there's no internal wiring.

When manufacturing died off in big cities such as New York and London, artists, musicians and other souls with a DIY ethos recognized the potential in the growing stock of empty—but often architecturally valuable and ruggedly beautiful—industrial and commercial buildings. They were renegades: Residing in industrial spaces was often illegal, particularly in the days before city governments calculated the benefits of gentrification and began to change zoning laws.

For those pioneers of the '60s and '70s, moving into a different model of architecture could also mean moving into an unorthodox model of living. Trading in suburban comfort for warehouse spaces may have introduced some compromises, but it also meant having the freedom to construct a less traditional, more personal version of domestic order. Living in an industrial space was both an aesthetic and cultural departure from the usual compartmentalized rooms designated for eating, sleeping and playing.

The unrefined beauty of such spaces bestows new qualities on otherwise ordinary contents. Plants tend to thrive, creating a counterpoint of botanical green. Pets, given extra space to play and hide, stake out personal territories, and there's a heightened aesthetic contrast between the smallness and softness of a human body and the industrial fabric around it.

Rather than being pushed up against walls, furniture takes center stage. It's used to define the space—the back of a sofa might become the permeable boundary between living area and kitchen, or a bookcase may pull double duty as a movable wall.

Windows in such spaces are often enormous and set in rows that take up entire walls. The changing light, which alternates between greenhouse-like and cinematic, becomes a key feature of the apartment: It wakes you up early, floods rooms during peak hours and renders the furniture's shadows as long-legged ghosts grazing on a field of wooden floorboards. At night, the space appears both larger and more intimate. Lamps create small pools of localized light, corners retreat into darkness and ceilings stretch up into dimly seen realms.

The unfinished surfaces of industrial-grade materials such as steel, wood and concrete, along with exposed pipes, columns and beams, give spaces a raw honesty that can only be accumulated over time, not acquired later as a superficial decoration. Records of their previous incarnations are present, as if someone had scrawled a message from the past in layers of exposed paint or lines across wooden floors where walls used to stand.

In this way, industrial spaces can be the template for imagining a different kind of life for ourselves. They make us wonder, "Are your dreams big enough to fill this space?"

JUNGYOU

CHOI

Although Jungyou Choi's home stands in a commercial district of Seoul amid a sea of flashing neon signs and towering buildings, living in the center of the city doesn't hinder her ability to create a serene sanctuary. "I'm the kind of person who needs a personal space most of the time," she says. "I can keep my life simple this way." Hidden from the street, the entrance to her modest second-floor home is accessible only through a side gate. This geographic feature almost instantly removes her from the commotion of the neighborhood. "It feels like an urban cottage," she says. "The house's interior was renovated using wood paneling, so it's like I'm surrounded by trees in a forest." In addition to these wooden features, natural light and soft materials create a warm atmosphere that influences the work she does as an independent designer. "My designs begin with what I feel and what I use, and my home is where it all happens. Everything I produce, I've tried in my home first," she says. With such a significant overlap between her work and home life, Jungyou makes a point to stay aware of the line between the two, though at times she finds it challenging. "Since I'm working at home, it's hard to separate my work from my personal life because I'm sitting in front of the computer and then doing the laundry a few minutes later," she says. "I'm not good at multitasking, but I have to work my way through it." Working days, evenings and weekends means Jungyou needs to maintain strong boundaries so she can leave time to relax. One trick she's learned is keeping her laptop out of her bedroom. "Now I have my sleeping place in the attic," she says. "It's a perfect place to escape where I don't work and truly rest." When she takes breaks during the day, she often escapes for hour-long bike rides along the Han River to enjoy a calm view of Seoul or spends afternoons being idle, savoring small details such as the light shifting across her walls. "The daylight is quite precious in my home, so I enjoy feeling the changes of the light throughout the day," she says. "The kitchen gets the most light, so I spend a lot of time there." Although Jungyou appreciates her home's natural elements, she has come to realize the value of material objects through her work designing products for other people's homes. She believes the trick to keeping the two worlds balanced is to keep around only items with character and personal connections that "touch your heart." Some of her most precious belongings include a collection of kitchen utensils she received from her mother. "Most of the tools and cups are older than I am," Jungyou says. "They give me such comfort and make me feel like I'm next to my mom all the time. They're like my little hometown."

In the following essay on page 244, we offer some suggestions on how to throw yourself an indulgent dinner party for one.

Above Left: Jungyou collaborated with a ceramist to design this collection, which is part of her "New Onggi" series. The various clays were steeped in lye and baked in an earthen kiln.

Right: Jungyou's favorite kitchen item is an aluminum kettle she purchased in Kathmandu, Nepal, where she worked for three months in 2013. She prepares her morning coffee with a beaker and a ceramic pour-over cup.

WORDS : NILS BERNSTEIN

SINGLE
SERVINGS

*Living alone doesn't mean you should be stuck with bland pasta
or a sad salad for dinner because there's no one else to impress.
Instead of eating for necessity, you should feel encouraged to whip
up a decadent three-course meal for yours truly.*

In her essay "On Dining Alone," famed food writer M.F.K. Fisher recounts the story of the Roman Empire gastronome Lucullus, who, when his servant defended serving a modest meal because there were no dinner guests, admonished, "It is precisely when I am alone that you require to pay special attention to the dinner. At such times, you must remember that Lucullus dines with Lucullus."

You should never think that cooking for yourself means there's no one to impress. Things that feel too extravagant or stressful for four—caviar or steak, for example—are perfect for one: six oysters are a treat, 24 a chore. Some dishes, such as risotto, stir-fries or spaghetti carbonara, are best when made in single portions. If you love to experiment in the kitchen, it's a time to try tricky dishes and techniques—spatchcocked chicken, béarnaise sauce, soufflé or caramel—in the safety of your own private sanctuary. This is also when you should enjoy those favorite dishes your loved ones don't care for (M.F.K. Fisher would take the opportunity to break out the canned shad roe, for example).

Rules go out the window: Eat breakfast for dinner, overdress your salad, have dessert first. As there's no one to witness your eating habits, you can enjoy some decadent culinary indulgences hunched over the sink as your amuse-bouche, such as a ripe mango slurped from its pit, sliced summer tomatoes or too much Gorgonzola on toasted pumpernickel.

For the delivery-prone, there are ways to make the idea of cooking solo seem less daunting: Choose dishes that can be prepared ahead of time and finished in the oven, preferably cooked in its serving dish, such as a small iron skillet or an oversize ramekin; use recipes as inspiration rather than doctrine, as repeatedly dividing ingredient lists by four is a drag; and shop at farmers markets, as this can spark creativity while allowing you to buy only what you need, and also at peak quality.

Still, like cashmere baby clothes or a manual typewriter, pleasure—not practicality—is the goal when throwing a dinner party for one. Don't worry about making extra in order to have leftovers (there's something naughty about making a single serving of soup from scratch). Why not make several tiny dishes for an antipasto platter, or two desserts if you can't decide between fruit and chocolate? You can fiddle leisurely around the kitchen all day or prep everything early and spend the rest of the afternoon reading cookbooks in bed.

When it's time to eat, though, take a break from your usual take-out tablescape. Even if it's your coffee table, set it with linens, your favorite dishes, a loose flower arrangement, beautiful bread and crisp radishes with the best butter and salt. Play lively music, but nothing too melancholy or loaded with nostalgia. Serve yourself in multiple courses. Eat slowly. Bathe. And Lucullus would want you to turn off your phone.

HOMES FOR SLOW LIVING

Living a slow lifestyle is about reclaiming time and spending it in whatever ways bring us happiness. Our homes are spaces where we can savor life on our own schedules and learn to become more aware of what we really want. Depending on what's important to us, home might be a sanctuary where mornings pass slowly and a three-hour breakfast in bed is the greatest sign of productivity, or we could while away afternoons looking out the window watching as clouds drift and leaves fall. If we crave more energy and adrenaline in our living environments, we might choose to challenge our dogs to a frenetic game of hide-and-seek or spend the morning working on projects from an office nook before having a homemade lunch on the couch. Although the following residents spend their time in various ways, they all follow their own natural rhythms. They've reset their internal clocks—and maybe even the clocks on the walls—to make sure their time is always focused on what matters most.

MIKKEL

& CAMILLA

KARSTAD

Unable to find the perfect home to accommodate their family of six, Mikkel and Camilla Karstad took matters into their own hands. The couple purchased two smaller units in a northern Copenhagen apartment complex and converted them into one spacious dwelling. Renovated with simplicity and practicality in mind, their home has an open layout and expansive windows that let in lots of natural light and provide stunning views of the city. To help them renovate, they enlisted the help of a young carpenter to design a functional and efficient kitchen inspired by Mikkel's years of working in the food industry as a chef, food stylist and cookbook author. As you might expect with a food-loving family, the Karstad clan's favorite room is the kitchen: "We spend a lot of time with the kids here doing homework, eating and talking," Mikkel says. "It's truly the heart of our home." They chose to raise their family in Copenhagen's Østerbro district because of its prime location and Camilla's attachment to the neighborhood. "Camilla was born and raised in this area, just on the other side of the lake," he says. "She loves the peaceful atmosphere, its proximity to downtown and all the relationships she has from her childhood." The couple and their four children—Oscar, Alma, Konrad and Viggo—live in a 1890s Ludvig Knudsen–designed building that was reportedly once home to a foundation for noble and royal Danish widows and their families. Although the duo leads busy lives—Mikkel runs the kitchen at a Danish law firm and Camilla works at a design agency—Sundays are set aside for

family bonding. "When I'm with my wife and kids, they're my number one priority, then work, then a social life and time for myself," Mikkel says. The family enjoys spending Sundays relaxing in their apartment, which is a quiet sanctuary away from the rush of city life. Mikkel and Camilla also love to take the kids swimming in one of the many nearby picturesque lakes or out of town on weekend foraging trips. "We find wild herbs in the spring, elderflower and rose hips in the summer, and berries, nuts and mushrooms in the autumn," Mikkel says. These ingredients often end up on the plates of their dinner guests, as they love to entertain and frequently have friends over for home-cooked meals and a good conversation. Mikkel usually takes the reins in the kitchen, whipping up an array of delicious recipes using local and seasonal ingredients. He credits his grandmother—who worked as a *kogekone* (cook) for many years—for passing down her culinary knowledge and nurturing his love of cooking. "We just hosted a private dinner for some friends where we made 12 dishes with winter vegetables and seafood," he says. At the heart of the couple's dinner parties is the desire to create a sense of warmth and community among their friends. "I want our guests to enjoy our home and company," Mikkel says. "I hope they feel like we've taken good care of them and know that they're always welcome."

In the following essay on page 258, we offer some advice on assembling a pantry that reflects your culinary heritage.

Left: The chair in Mikkel and Camilla's hallway is a Hans J. Wegner design. The large artwork is by Copenhagen-based artist Tal R and the smaller one is by John Kørner. The lamp is by Arne Jacobsen, and a eucalyptus plant is perched on the windowsill.

Above Right: Mikkel holds a bowl with a simple winter fish dish of fried cod with baked leeks, capers and dill. His favorite utensils are a good sharp knife and a tablespoon to taste his cooking as he goes along.

WORDS : ALICA FORNERET

CULINARY
COMMODITIES

Whether your kitchen is the heart of your home or a place where quick meals are zapped in a microwave, there are plenty of reasons to keep more than dried pasta on hand. A few chefs share their thoughts about how to stock a pantry with ingredients that'll make any home cook feel prepared.

Heritage

Because some of us have a weakness for exotic salts while others have addictions to spicy condiments, our pantries should similarly reflect our personal preferences. What we consider to be staples goes far beyond dry goods, olive oil and lemons, and while many chefs tout the importance of keeping a good hunk of Parmesan on hand, this cheesy addition won't bode well for those who prefer to cook with miso paste or kaffir leaves. Our pantries should therefore contain the ingredients every home cook needs to feel comfortable in the kitchen. Incorporating these elements into the home pantry ensures a connection rooted in your culinary heritage. Chef Brent Tranchina, a native New Orleanian, has been influenced by his roots in both Trinidad and Louisiana. "Essential ingredients represent our personal stories, upbringings and heritage," he says. Growing up, his dinner table menu ranged from spicy curries to gumbos, which meant his family had a fully stocked spice department. "My mom would make Trinidadian curry with chicken, goat or shrimp and would use a common curry powder packet by Chief, a brand from Trinidad," Brent says. "I love the flavors in that packet, but it can be hard to find, so I'm often left with having to make my own curry powder with the same ingredients I always have in the house."

Inspiration

In one corner of every pantry hides a dusty can of beans or a box of polenta that's being saved for an emergency—items kept around for rainy days or when you're too busy to run to the store. When your supply closet has been eaten down to its final ingredients, these bland, mass-produced items are often ironically stored next to bottles of odd specialty items you bought for a single obscure dish and never used again. Combining the ordinary with the rarely used extraordinary can spark culinary experimentation (and also makes use of the remnants of those expensive one-off purchases). Cheesemonger Yoav Perry always has the fixings for a creative cheese plate handy and considers it an excuse to try out new pairings and clean out some exotic items. "What good is a cheese plate if you don't visit your pantry first?" he says. "It's the perfect excuse to use marmalades, chutneys, fancy pickles, mustards and honey." To stay on top of your supply, take stock of your inventory, rotate goods from the back to the front of your shelves and try to eat through your entire supply of goodies once a year so you can replace them with new ones.

Quality

By learning a few simple canning and pickling methods, you'll have many options for keeping quality ingredients on hand year-round (and you can also enjoy seasonal fruits when they're no longer available at the market). Sourcing ingredients for canning when they're in season guarantees the quality of your long-term preserves. "Making your own jam at home when the fruit is in its prime means having a jam on hand with vibrancy," says Jessica Koslow, jam-maker extraordinaire of Los Angeles restaurant Sqirl. She believes that a pantry should be filled with items that equally honor your body, local bounty and the folks you're cooking for.

Three chefs share their essential pantry staples, along with the items they cannot live without.

NICK KORBEE, EGG SHOP, NEW YORK CITY:
ESSENTIAL ITEMS: Blue steel pans, citrus juicer, Maille extra-hot smooth Dijon mustard and a sourdough starter.
NONESSENTIAL ITEMS: Husk cherries and blue cheese.

KRISTEN MURRAY, MÂURICE, PORTLAND, OREGON:
ESSENTIAL ITEMS: Good butter, farm eggs, citrus, vanilla, rosemary and local fruits, vegetables and nuts.
NONESSENTIAL ITEMS: Oysters and raspberries.

JUSTIN BURKE-SAMSON, PARTY OF TWO, BOSTON, MASSACHUSETTS:
ESSENTIAL ITEMS: Two commercial KitchenAid mixers, a cake tester and an endless supply of powdered sugar.
NONESSENTIAL ITEMS: Corn Flakes and marshmallows.

YUKIKO

KURODA

From a quick glimpse, Yukiko Kuroda's home appears to be located in Japan's wooded countryside, but it's actually nestled between tall trees in a crowded inner-Tokyo neighborhood. Although it was built after World War II, it reflects the ancestral wisdom and cultural climate of a much older mode of traditional Japanese architecture. "I made a choice to incorporate Japanese traditions into this modern life," Yukiko says. She loves the texture of the tatami floors beneath her feet and the soft light that filters through the *shōji*-paper dividing walls. However, Yukiko doesn't understand why her ancestors thought paper was a savvy material for the construction of walls: "It's too easily broken by a finger or an enemy, like a samurai rushing through your house," she says, laughing. "Why didn't they choose a stronger material? It fascinates me." For some time now it's been customary in Japan to build a house designed to withstand the height of summer—Yukiko doesn't own an air conditioner, but even if she wanted one, most areas of her home don't have enough electricity to run simple appliances. She believes we can live a comfortable life without such modern amenities; she simply lets the wind whistle through the house instead of relying on man-made devices, and microwaves and refrigerators aren't daily essentials

in her kitchen. Instead, she pulls up cool water from the well on her property, uses ventilated bamboo baskets to keep produce fresh and pickles or ferments perishable items, storing them in tall jars in her pantry. "How you eat and how you live leads to how you exist," she says. "I believe from the bottom of my heart that if I waste food, nature or anything else, then I'll pay for it someday." Her desire to repair rather than replace extends to her work in *kintsugi*, which is the traditional Japanese craft of fixing broken pottery using sap called *urushi* that's made with ingredients such as dirt, rice and powdered gold. Instead of trying to hide the cracks in these ancient pieces, the gold highlights the pottery's flaws and acts as a nod of recognition to the past. Through applying the concept of *wabi-sabi* (an appreciation for the imperfect and temporal nature of things) to both her work and domestic life, she sticks to her ethos down to the smallest elements of her daily rituals. Because of this, her bond with her home is particularly strong. "I respect my home a lot and regard it as my mentor," she says. "I'm a pupil of my house."

In the following essay on page 266, we consider how people living in the center of big cities can find moments of calm.

Left: Yukiko has many favorite kitchen utensils, but she likes ones made out of wood and bamboo the most. She doesn't have a particular attachment to certain brands or products and only cares for objects that are simple, honest and reliable.

Above: Yukiko's late mother once used this basket for her groceries. The large ceramic bowl was made in the Tōhoku region of Japan: Yukiko uses it to make pickled vegetables.

WORDS : ANNU SUBRAMANIAN

A SANCTUARY
IN THE CITY

Creating an oasis of calm in a towering urban metropolis may be challenging, but by slightly changing the way we think, we can learn to appreciate the advantages of both the rapid and slow paces of life.

Life in a city can be electric, fast and crowded. Whenever we step out of our urban homes, we join a network that's packed with opportunities. The chances to grow and expand can feel endless, even if at times we can hardly stretch our arms out across the sidewalk. The flip side to having the city's untapped wonders at our fingertips is that its energy can be exhausting and leave us craving a slower and quieter pace, one where we can roam unencumbered or savor a meal without a waiter asking, "You still working on that?"

Instead of shunning one mode of energy in favor of the other, we can learn how to perch in the middle ground with the quiet hum of our sanctuary in one ear and the blaze of an ambulance siren in the other. Some may call it compromise, but it's best to consider it a kind of balance in contrasts.

Building a slow lifestyle in a fast-paced city feels all the better for its incongruousness, kind of like how stepping into a hot shower is much more satisfying when it's cold outside. We might not be able to plant rows of vegetables on a large plot of land, but we can grow herbs in pots on windowsills. We might not have access to the grounding quiet of an empty country lane, but we can silence our phones and turn up some jazz on a weekend morning.

In terms of decor, reducing clutter and making space for natural light to pour through our open windows draws us closer to something organic. Home doesn't have to be a place where we arrange all-new "reclaimed" wood furniture to create a contrived sense of shabby chic: Whether we build our headboards from found objects or use an Allen wrench to connect panels like many before us, when we put together the elements of our space, it gives us a sense of pride and a feeling of humble accomplishment.

Finding a bit of provincial solace in a city-bound home doesn't have to mean solitude, though. Instead, we can partake in the long-table lore of country life in our own living rooms, even if that means a few people wind up perched on trunks or milk crates. Take note of how your conversations change when they don't take place over expensive cocktails and urban din. Joining friends in their homes can make for evenings that move according to their own timetables without the presence of hovering servers silently nudging you to pay the check.

Best of all, crafting a rustic lifestyle brings calm into our own sanctums. It diffuses the pressures of the outside world so that we feel relieved as we cross the threshold into our homes. We can't control everything that happens outside—from lengthy bus delays to angry sidewalk-sharers—but we can find some peace and perspective in our spaces. Whether we come home to fall asleep or tackle a to-do list as tea cools beside us, we find joy in a serene space that prepares us for our next departure into the outside world.

The opportunity to have a slower domestic lifestyle within the city allows us to appreciate the streets' hectic and intoxicating pace even more. By introducing a quieter, less hurried routine to our urban setting, we may achieve the best of both worlds: We can just as quickly visit a museum, pick up fusion cuisine from a food truck and rush to a swing-dancing party as we can spend an afternoon simmering stock and writing letters. We might not have the best view of the stars, but we can still look out at the bright lights of our skyline and feel content.

ALYSON FOX

& DEREK

DOLLAHITE

"We were outgrowing our house in Austin and wanted a bit more breathing room," says designer Alyson Fox about relocating with her husband to Spicewood, Texas, a rural town about an hour away from the state capital of Austin. After picking out a plot of land and deciding to build their house from the ground up, Alyson and Derek enlisted their families' help with the lengthy construction process: Alyson's father-in-law drew up the floor plans and her brother-in-law acted as the general contractor and outfitted much of the house with custom woodwork. She's convinced it would've been trickier without the entire clan chipping in: "There was so much to consider, so we knew it would've been impossible for the process not to be stressful and tiring. But when the inevitable arguments ensue, at least they're with the people you love!" she says, laughing. Alyson and Derek, who is a creative director working in advertising, designed their home's layout to integrate and honor the raw beauty of the surrounding landscape. "We tried to create a space that was about the land we're on and kept the design elements simple so the two could work alongside each other," Alyson says. The interior features large glass windows, high ceilings, an open-plan kitchen, a huge collection of Alyson's indoor potted plants—which she admits she has a weakness for—and lots of exposed storage. The concrete floor is kept relatively bare and walls are largely unadorned, which directs

visitors to gaze at the seemingly endless bushland right outside their door. "The whole space is about finding the right balance between opposites, like old and new, warm and clean, function and beauty." Alyson and Derek spend much of their time working from home, and they try to structure each workday like a typical day at the office, with a set morning schedule that accommodates breaks for lunch and playing with their puppy, Stache. "With the exception of our dog barking when he looks out the window and happens to see a deer, a fox or a road-runner's weird strut, it's a very quiet place to live," Derek says. The sense of peace offered by their rural location also helps stimulate their creative processes, and they love the intimacy of living in a small community. Although there isn't much in the way of restaurants and entertainment near their remote home, the former city dwellers have grown to embrace their newfound rural life: Some of their favorite moments here have been spent simply sitting together at the kitchen table taking in their surroundings. "It's been really nice to kind of fall into the natural pattern of sunrises and seasons," Alyson says. "I don't think I ever knew what a thunderstorm actually looked like until we moved here."

In the following guide on page 276, we offer a few suggestions for keeping your houseplants as healthy and happy as Alyson's greenery.

Previous Page: Alyson and Derek enjoy playing catch with their puppy, Stache, in the long hallway or having a game of hide-and-seek in the fields outside.

Left: Alyson found the vintage boucherouite rug that's hanging on the wall on Etsy at the beginning of their building process. She designed the bedside table as part of her Shapes Stool Series. Some of the books sitting on it are *We Tell Ourselves Stories in Order to Live* by Joan Didion and *We Others* by Steven Millhauser. Alyson and Derek are also fans of Unison Home sheets, wool blankets and linen coverlets.

Above: Alyson's favorite kitchen items include a Staub kettle, a John Boos chopping block, Mazama ceramics and a cast-iron spice grinder she found in Seattle. She loves whipping up salt-baked fish, roasted potatoes or anything taco-related with Derek's homemade salsa.

Above Right: The plants in their home include a curly willow tree, assorted succulents, a fig tree, rubber plants and a kumquat tree. Alyson confesses to having a particular obsession with bringing plants home.

WORDS : ELIZA BLANK

A GUIDE FOR
BLACK THUMBS

Filling our homes with an array of potted plants can enhance the feel-good vibes, but we also need to learn how to keep both them and the atmosphere alive. Here's some expert advice on cultivating your greenery without creating a succulent graveyard.

Face the Light

Determine how much sunlight gets into your home and choose your plants accordingly. Don't forget to take into consideration if there's something outside the window that may obstruct the light, such as a tree or a wall. The best place to start is figuring out which direction your windows face.

— SOUTH-FACING ROOMS: These rooms get bright light for the majority of the day in the northern hemisphere (it's the opposite in the south). Choose almost any plant and arrange them a few feet from the windows. Try cacti, alocasias and flowering or fruit-bearing plants such as oxalis, begonias or dwarf Meyer lemon trees.

— EAST- AND WEST-FACING ROOMS: These rooms are filled with a medium amount of light for the majority of the day, but still keep your plants within a few feet of the window—we recommend pilea, peperomia, palms, dracaena, ficus or ferns.

— NORTH-FACING ROOMS: These rooms receive the least light if you live up north, so choose plants that can endure low-light conditions and keep them directly on the windowsill. Some suggestions include pothos, philodendrons, arrowheads, Chinese evergreens, peace lilies and zamioculcas (or "ZZ").

Be Realistic

Be sure to consider your daily schedule, travel frequency and general forgetfulness when you decide on a plant. If your absentmindedness is what stands in the way of plant ownership, try a succulent or a cactus—they store water in their leaves, stems and even roots, enabling them to survive periods of drought and distress. Truly, the only way to kill either of these is overcare! Our favorite succulent is, and always will be, the jade.

Throw Some Shade

While you want to provide sunlight for your plant, be careful to protect it from intense direct rays: If the sun is powerful enough to scorch your skin, it's certainly too much for your plant's leaves. To protect them from burning, draw a sheer curtain across the window or move them a foot away from the window.

Don't Overlove

Beware of overwatering: It's the easiest way to kill a plant. You may be tempted to water your plant on a schedule, but it's best to water it only when needed. Always check the soil first before giving it a drink: If the soil is darker in color and sticks to your finger, the plant should be fine for the time being. If you're a novice, also stay away from fertilizer—it's another accidental way to kill your plant. Plants get minerals from the air, water and potting mix and are nourished by sunlight, so it's entirely possible to have a healthy plant without additives.

Soak It Up

To water your plant, gently lift the foliage and flood the potting mix with tepid water until a trickle appears from the drainage hole at the bottom. Let the plant soak up the water for 30 minutes, then empty any remaining water from the saucer. If your planter doesn't have a drainage hole at the bottom to allow excess water to escape from the soil, it's important to create makeshift drainage. You can do this by lining the bottom of the planter with rocks and sand—this added precaution will also help you avoid overwatering your plants.

Turn Up the Heat

As with humans, plants are most comfortable between 65 and 75 degrees Fahrenheit (18 and 24 degrees Celsius). Avoid placing your plant near temperature hazards such as vents, radiators and exterior doors, which may create hot or cold spots and drafts. If you like plants that prefer more humid conditions such as ferns, ivies or tropical plants, mist them using a small spray bottle every few days. During the dry months of winter, also group your plants together to help create a humid microclimate.

Consult an Expert

It's best to buy quality plants from knowledgeable experts at local nurseries, garden centers and florists. Definitely give your plant a once-over before purchasing—watch out for yellowed leaves, fungal diseases such as powdery mildew, leaf spots, brown leaf tips, weak or wobbly stems and other obvious signs of poor plant health.

TAKAHIRO

& REIKO

KINOSHITA

Considering that Takahiro Kinoshita's busy schedule as the editor in chief of the Tokyo-based fashion magazine *POPEYE* involves frequent overseas trips for work, he treasures the moments he gets to spend at home with his family. He and his wife, Reiko, live in an apartment just outside Tokyo's city center with their two young sons, Akiharu and Haruma. When they purchased their home, the couple outfitted their living room with oak walls to inject more classic and organic elements into the modern apartment. "I feel like our apartment achieves a sense of harmony between old and new," Takahiro says. "While I really like mid-century design, I tend to mix furniture from that era with contemporary items to ensure a balance in my home." Their apartment also includes large east-facing windows that let in lots of natural light, which provides Takahiro with an ideal environment in which to relax, unwind or mull over his many projects in a setting other than the office. "Working in the publishing industry means I'm constantly seeking inspiration or thinking about my work, whether it's through movies, books or even when spending time with family," he says. "I do think it's important to relax as much as possible when I'm at home, but I often gain inspiration and new ideas for *POPEYE* from my home life." While his editorial work has made him an influential trendsetter both in Japan and abroad, he takes a

deliberately old-fashioned approach to home decor. His interior design taste has been largely influenced by his *senpai*—a respectful Japanese term for your elders, often in a work or school environment—he met when he was younger. "One particular senpai had a room furnished purely with art deco pieces," he says. "He taught me how to choose items, arrange furniture and even find a house. While my taste tends more toward mid-century furniture rather than the art deco style, I still think of this senpai when designing my home." Since having children, the couple has started to lean more toward choosing functional, beautiful and long-lasting items that can endure the wear and tear of two little ones running around. Their older son Akiharu's favorite part of the home is the large tent his parents set up in the living room where he likes playing with his father when he comes home from work. "The rooms in this house used to just be for us adults, so I'm looking forward to creating more spaces for our children," Takahiro says. After a frantic day at the office, he loves nothing more than returning home to his family, which he describes as the center of his life. "I'm fortunate to choose the work I like, to live in a wonderful home and to be surrounded by family that I love," he says. "These three things are the most important aspects of my life."

IN THE SIXTIES

ohs by Glen Denny

LERY · YOSEMITE NATIONAL PARK

2007 - JANUARY 2008

Yosemite Climbing Association

Left: The tent is a Hubba HP tent by MSR. Takahiro purchased the Navajo rug in Santa Fe, New Mexico, and the flowers hanging from the ceiling are mimosas. Takahiro and Reiko's son Akiharu is currently obsessed with planes.

Above: Takahiro found this wooden toy car in Scandinavia. The 1950s coffee table was designed by architect Eero Saarinen.

Right: The various art pieces propped up against the wall include a vintage print by Umetaro Azechi, a photograph by Tahakiro's friend Kazuhiro Fujita and a vintage print by Paul Colin. The wooden blocks on the windowsill are designed by All the Way to Paris for HAY.

EMMA

& JOAKIM

OLBERS

Emma and Joakim Olbers' family splits its time between two incredibly different homes: a sprawling wooden house off the coast of Stockholm and a centrally located city apartment. "For me, it's a perfect mix," Emma says. She enjoys the quick pace and convenience of the city, but she also finds peace in the archipelago's serenity. "Being in the country with nature and quiet is where I get time off, time to not think," she says. "I have a hard time choosing, so I need the balance of both. I feel at home in both places." These worlds shape Emma's work as a furniture designer through her attention to the natural elements present in daily life. She takes the influence of her time spent in the woods—she loves to be in the forest making campfires and chopping firewood for the winter—and applies it to both her designs and the way she fills her family's apartment in Stockholm. Emma prides herself on being "a furniture designer with an eco heart," as her process starts and ends with the environment in mind. "I usually begin by thinking about what's going to happen at the end of a product's life and how it's going to be recycled," she says. Emma and Joakim have made a conscious effort to use eco-friendly products in both of their homes. Sofas and storage units were all thoughtfully sourced from sustainable designers or from Emma's collection, including their front hallway bench: "It's made of birch that's grown and chopped just two hours away from the factory, and the coating that finishes it is an egg tempera, which is a paint that consists only of egg, pigments, flax oil and water," she says. While their commitment to staying green is paramount to the choices they make in their homes, Emma and Joakim's desire to create environments that are durable and mindful of their two young sons, Fabian and Julius, is also of utmost importance. As the kids have grown older and the homes' furniture has evolved, they have remained focused on functional pieces for their sons' sake. "As a furniture designer, function is always at the forefront of my mind," Emma says. "That includes the furniture being able to take the wear and tear of having children around."

In the following essay on page 292, we celebrate how the less-than-perfect aspects of a well-worn home can bring a family together.

Above Right: Emma's family loves having taco dinners at their kitchen table. She designed the light fixtures in the kitchen and one of the candlestick holders is from Skultuna, a 16th-century Swedish brass foundry.

Right: The images on the wall are pages from an old nature book that was passed down to Emma from her grandmother.

WORDS : DANIELLE DEMETRIOU

BETTER
WITH AGE

*Like a fine bottle of cabernet, most houses improve with a little time
on their side. Instead of fixating on the negative aspects of the scratches
and flaws that characterize a seasoned home, we should appreciate
the marks that make memories.*

There's a particular beauty to be admired in homes that are allowed to age gracefully and show the wear and tear of everyday life. Fragments of beauty can be spied in the most mundane quotidian objects: the gentle sagging of a sofa, the frayed edges of a handmade quilt, the symphonic creaks of wooden floorboards and the lazy creases of white bed linen.

Lived-in homes seem to evolve harmoniously with their inhabitants. They become a sort of three-dimensional domestic diary where each mark, scratch and crack records a secret, a memory, an emotion or a story. The patina of a weathered wooden tabletop can reveal the laughter and shared intimacies of wine-drenched dinner parties or a child's cereal-spilling breakfasts.

In an era where perfection is endlessly sought (for our bodies, our wardrobes, our social-media personas), a home that celebrates a well-lived life is one to be appreciated. Such a home is the antithesis of the near-clinical shininess found inside the walls of uniform interior-design stores, the pages of glossy decor magazines and the rose-tinted world of commercials on television.

A home that's given the space to age at its own pace can provide the perfect backdrop for the unfolding chaos of our days. Take the kitchen, for example: The roasting pans may be blackened from Sunday lunches, the cookbooks splashed with traces of new meals and memories being made, the herb boxes overflowing and the wooden worktop tattooed with abstract scrapes. A quick peek in the bedroom may reveal shafts of light filtering through sunshine-faded curtains while the much-loved woven rug in the sitting room might be worn down through the endless imprints of passing footsteps.

The concept of appreciating time and nature's ability to add deeper meaning to our lives isn't new. In some cultures, objects that have become worn with love are often praised more highly than those that are shiny and new. The Japanese are particularly keen believers of this line of thinking, as reflected in their deep awareness of *wabi-sabi*, a concept that savors the flawed, the imperfect, the weathered—from the uneven edge of a chipped ceramic teacup to the wind-beaten facade of an old wooden house. In this case, beauty isn't confined to the purely physical form of an object, but instead expands to the intangible—the atmosphere and the feeling of our belongings and of our spaces.

The owners of any living, breathing space have a choice: They can engage in a perpetual struggle for perfectionism with endless efforts to maintain a permanent state of absolute tidiness, or they can stop and savor the imperfections. There's joy to be found in celebrating these details rather than airbrushing them out of existence. A home doesn't need to be perfectly pristine at all times—a little messiness is a microcosm of the disorder of life itself, and a sign of a warm and welcoming home is that it looks as lived-in as it is loved.

So bring on the wall scribbles from overzealous toddlers, the pile of books with dog-eared pages and the frayed straw basket full of vegetables in the kitchen. Add to this mix a cast of residents and visitors, and you have a home that grows more beautiful with every moment.

CARIN SCHEVE

& FRANCESCO

CARAMELLA

The views of Manhattan from Carin Scheve and Francesco Caramella's Brooklyn apartment are hard to beat: "Our windows face the Hudson River and the Statue of Liberty, and we get the most beautiful sunsets," says Carin, an interior and prop stylist. "It gives us the impression of being on the waterfront even though we live in a very industrial area." Carin and Francesco live with their son, Milo, in a building in Sunset Park that used to function as a storage space for one of the manufacturing, warehousing and shipping trades operating in their neighborhood. "Our area was one of the first intermodal shipping complexes in the United States," Carin says. "Now the neighborhood attracts a lot of artists and photographers because of the great light and large warehouse units available for rent." The layout of the couple's home mirrors the area's industrial feel with concrete floors, steel windows and concrete columns designed to prop up high ceilings. While the couple preserved much of the original open floor plan, a few walls were erected throughout the house to create separate spaces for work and living. "The cavernous layout of the loft creates a wonderful echo and has great acoustics. We sometimes host small concerts in our home," Carin says. She and Francesco are driven by their creative professions—he works as an architect but often helps her source vintage furniture and props—and are constantly modifying both the structure and layout of the abode. "My work represents a way of living, so I'm always on the lookout for new ideas to switch up my home," she says. "I remember changing my childhood room every month or so because I was fascinated by how I could make it feel different by modifying a few elements." Living in such an expansive apartment allows them to seamlessly integrate their personal and professional lives; both frequently work from home and have been able to hold photo shoots there without having to rearrange all the furniture. "We often build, design and work in this space, so it's the perfect place to mix work and play," Carin says. "We have more than enough room to host large numbers of people and the space readily adapts to our every need." Carin and Francesco have also taken measures to soften their home's rugged structure by adding furniture and home wares that have a deep emotional resonance and provide a touch of warmth. "One of my favorite pieces is the rocking chair I got right before Milo was born," she says. "I've spent countless hours in it rocking him to sleep."

Previous Page: Carin and Francesco's tea set is from Royal Holland and the salad bowl is by Tom Dixon. She found the artwork that hangs on the wall in the vintage section of Manhattan store Fishs Eddy.

Left: Carin salvaged the copper light shades at a vintage market, and Francesco designed their dining table. The collection of chairs that surround it includes pieces from Arne Jacobsen, Crate & Barrel and Eames.

MIRKO BEETSCHEN

& STÉPHANE

HOULMANN

Mirko Beetschen and Stéphane Houlmann's partnership is both professional and domestic: They founded a company together and also divide their time between Zurich and the waterside town of Interlaken in central Switzerland. "Interlaken is like going back to my roots, which I'd never originally planned to do, but it feels good," Mirko says. Bergdorf Homes, their interior design and journalism business, keeps them connected to their office and apartment in Zurich, and while Mirko loves the city, he's fully aware of the benefits provided by both environments. "I wouldn't want to be in Interlaken constantly," he says. "I need the city— at least for some moments—but I'm not in Zurich with my full heart." Their home in Interlaken is surrounded by classic chalets and villas that date back to the 19th and 20th centuries. With Alpine tourism booming in the 1890s, many travelers spent their summers in the area and rented farmhouses such as theirs as vacation spots. When they first found their home, it was located on a property in a lush meadow hidden behind overgrown bushes and trees. "It really was love at first sight," Mirko says. But when they inquired about it, they discovered it had already been purchased. Fortunately for Mirko and Stéphane, when the home's original investors found out that the house couldn't be demolished because the Swiss government had designated it as a cultural landmark, the duo passed by the property a year later to find it unchanged and

available again. "During our first visit, we discovered a veritable treasure box of beautiful old rooms," Mirko says. "The uniqueness of the house, its homeyness and beautiful original structure attracted us." The space is now a peaceful place where they both feel at home—as do the constant stream of vacationers that often join them on their weekend trips to Interlaken. The variety of nooks and rooms allows up to 14 people to stay in the house at once, and the couple is most often joined by a friend and her two boys, who are Mirko and Stéphane's godchildren. They enjoy spending time in the kitchen, and some of their fondest memories are of evenings spent over the stove. "Once when we first purchased the house, we were in the middle of renovating and felt like celebrating," Mirko says. "The heat wasn't working yet, but the old tiled stove in the dining room was already restored. So we made a fire to warm up, I cleaned the area that had been full of dust and dirt, and Stéphane cooked in the kitchen. Luckily, we already had some of the furniture. The whole thing felt a bit like [1987 Danish film] *Babette's Feast*, and ever since then, we've tried to keep this Puritan, serene atmosphere in the dining room."

In the following guide on page 310, we offer some suggestions for planning the perfect stay-at-home vacation.

Above Left: Mirko and Stéphane's cat, Elliot, loves the little nooks and crannies in the house and out on the terrace. His favorite room is the summer room—an unheated, enclosed section of the veranda with a chaise lounge.

WORDS : GEORGIA FRANCES KING

A GUIDE TO
STAYCATIONS

While everyone else competes for limited highway space this weekend,
why not just turn your home into the ideal space for a dream staycation?
This guide will help you and your family take a vacation without opening
your wallet or car door.

Times may be tough, but finding time is even tougher. If you're struggling to grab more than a few days off or digging down between the couch pillows looking for loose change, here is a word that might come in handy: staycation. No bedbug-infested hotel rooms, no knee-cramping flights, no slimy travel agents—just you, your abode and your stay-at-home vacation. The trick is to fool yourself into feeling like you've been transported to a nostalgic wonderland, not just the other end of your living room. While pillow forts will never grow old (at least as long as there's a bottle of merlot involved), here are a few ideas for grown-up staycations that bring new meaning to a "home away from home."

Break Routine

The first step to a successful staycation is eradicating your daily habits and re-creating the kinds you might form if waking up to a mai tai and a foot rub every day. Granola may be a hassle-free breakfast option, but try making yourself a fancy cooked brunch in bed (better yet, get someone else to make it for you). After straightening your sheets, place a comically sized chocolate on your pillow for you to miraculously find later in the day. Fold the end of your toilet paper down into those nifty little triangles. Wash using only individual gourmet soaps. By tricking yourself into thinking you're not at home, you'll be less likely to start puttering about and reorganizing your linen closet.

Dine Out

You know that little Italian joint around the corner? The one with the gingham tablecloths that look like Dorothy got lost on her way to Oz? The one you never normally go to because you figure you can just make pasta at home? Go there. But don't head out in jeans and a T-shirt—get dressed up. Be the best-dressed person in that tiny trattoria, just short of wearing a full-length ball gown. Order a bottle of Chianti. Bring your own candles. Reenact scenes from *Lady and the Tramp*. Making the familiar seem exotic is a staycation must.

Or Dine In

Some recipes require several days and a whole lot of patience to bring to fruition—and that means several successive days you don't typically have to spend in the kitchen up to your elbows in dough. So have a whirl at curing your own meat or fish. Soak a variety of dried grains. Make your own puff pastry. Take some time to master the dishes your grandparents made from scratch, and enjoy these lengthy methods instead of trying to speed up things. If you want to take your culinary holiday to the next level, get creative and theme every day's meals around a different concept—like a country or a color—and munch only on foodstuff relating to that notion.

Get Out of Town

Getting out of the house for a sojourn is a fine way to stave off staycation-induced cabin fever. Take yourself on a day trip (just not the type the Beatles sung about) by finding a quaint place a few hours out of town, packing a picnic lunch and pioneering your own surroundings. An advantage of taking day trips is you get to go home at sundown instead of finding a dodgy roadside motel with more flickering neon lights than an early-'90s rave. Go fruit picking, visit a distant cookie-bearing relative or set out to spend five bucks in every thrift shop within a five-mile radius. Head to the tourist spot you always felt too silly to visit and force yourself to take the cheesiest photograph possible. To make your day-holiday feel authentic, send your friend a postcard, even if it's just from a pub two towns over. And the best, most cockle-warming part? By staying close to home, you're revitalizing local small businesses. High five.

Or Stay In

If you can't muster the motivation to get out of your pajamas and face the outside world, there are plenty of ways to transform your home into a resort with its own activity schedule. If you have a balcony or a backyard, buy a blow-up pool and invite some friends over for a paddle. Search the bookshelves for a dusty set of dominoes and try to remember the rules (or make up new ones). Create a bowling alley in your hallway using toilet rolls and a tennis ball. Find an old projector, whip out a sheet and set up your own indoor cinema, complete with fresh popcorn. The biggest rule is to avoid doing anything you'd do on an average weekend, lest you head back to the daily grind on Monday feeling like you've wasted your staycation attempting to resist cleaning the gutters. That means no *Seinfeld* marathons, no vacuuming and no standing in front of the fridge eating peanut butter with a spoon. Well, at least not every day.

MOMO SUZUKI

& ALEXANDER

YAMAGUCHI

Momo Suzuki carries her passion for natural fabrics and minimalist design home from work. The Japanese-born fashion designer and cofounder of the independent clothing label Black Crane lives with her husband, fellow designer Alexander Yamaguchi, in the Pasadena neighborhood of Los Angeles. After purchasing their home from the original architect's family, they carried out renovations that preserved the original cabinetry and large windows—elements that initially attracted them to the property. "Sometimes better solutions emerge from respecting the current conditions of the space instead of changing everything," Momo says. "We kept 'simple and functional' as our mantra when renovating our home." Momo and Alexander took down the wall separating the living and dining rooms to create a more spacious area and widened the opening between the kitchen and dining room so they could interact with guests while cooking. They also made use of different materials to add more depth and texture to the interior— including ceramic tiles, oak and walnut wood furnishings and natural fabrics such as linen and cotton—and they gave the wood elements only a light finishing coat to let them age naturally. "I love subtle gestures and imperfect beauty, both of which can be created by appreciating the effect of time passing," Momo says. She and Alexander have similar aesthetic

philosophies when it comes to interior design and enjoy hunting for unusual pieces at flea markets and local furniture dealers. "We both love the concept of timeless, effortless and relaxed decor," she says. "We often sit together on the couch with a cup of tea, looking around the house and discussing what we want to change next." While Momo's taste tends toward the minimalist end of the spectrum, Alexander is more adventurous in weaving different textural elements into the fabric of their house through his assortment of artisanal objects: His extensive collection includes works by ceramic artist Stan Bitters and wood sculptures by Hideki Takayama and Alma Allen. The couple's most treasured items are the steel handles on their front doors, which were a gift from their close friend Yasushi and his wife, jewelry designer Satomi Kawakita. "Yasushi inlaid a very delicate and beautiful gold line in each steel door handle that reminds me of Satomi's jewelry designs," Momo says. "We touch these handles every day—they remind us of the great friendship we have." Although Momo and Alexander's many projects keep them busy, long days begin and end at home with two of their favorite activities: lingering over relaxing breakfasts as the morning light pours through their kitchen window and browsing books in the living room while watching the sun set.

Left: Momo and Alexander's Viesso sofa is complemented by a Milo Baughman chair, a Kneeland Mercado rug and a coffee table designed by Poul Kjærholm. Both the artwork and the ceramics on the cabinet are vintage.

JOANNA LAVÉN

& DAVID

WAHLGREN

Joanna Lavén and David Wahlgren's quiet fifth-floor apartment looks out over the streets of Östermalm, a calm residential area of Stockholm. Although the home they share with their daughters, Elise and Julie, is a refuge, city life isn't far away: The streets of their neighborhood below are lined with a number of shops and parks, and the zoo that their children like to visit isn't too far away either. "I love being in the city—the atmosphere when you walk out of the building with life buzzing everywhere," Joanna says. When they moved to this part of town, the couple was immediately drawn to both the local community and the setup of their new abode: Originally built by architect H. Westerlund between 1913 and 1918, their apartment features a balcony and a large social area facing the street. When it came to decorating, it was easy for the duo to collaborate after living together for 14 years. "Fortunately we have the same taste, and that taste has developed over the years," Joanna says. Since, as a stylist, she experiments with colors all day, she favors neutral, calm shades of paint at home. This also allows her to focus on setting an atmosphere that doesn't feel overstyled. "It's more relaxing to keep the aesthetic simple in our apartment," she says. Although David works as a programmer, he is passionate about interiors, so furnishing the home together was an opportunity to build a personal space that reflected both of their approaches toward design. They did most of their furniture sourcing through online auctions and prefer pieces with history and strength. "I love that you don't have to contribute to the mass production of things that people buy and throw away after a few years," Joanna says. After helping decorate multiple children-filled homes through her work, she has recognized that long-term durability reigns supreme, but you also have to let some of the little things slide. "I like to keep everything that's visible tidy, but I don't have a superclean floor," she says. "There might be some breadcrumbs under the kitchen table, but that doesn't bother me." By accepting the messy realities of living in an apartment with small kids, the couple has come to realize the essential elements of family life. "The most important qualities a home must possess are a location you love and enough space for your family," Joanna says, "and a nice kitchen is a big plus."

Above: A lamp by Jieldé sits in Joanna and David's
bedroom and a Swedish painter and sculptor named Lennart
Sand painted the artwork on the wall. She bought the latter at
an auction and reframed it to suit the bedroom.

Following Page: The Sunburst Wall Clock is by George
Nelson and the candlestick holders are by Gunnar Ander for
Ystad Metall.

Left: Albert Johansson, a Swedish minimalist painter and one of Joanna's favorite artists, painted the artwork that hangs in the living room. The light fixture is a Venini creation from the 1960s.

MIKE & CONNY

KARLSSON

LUNDGREN

After years of splitting their time between Berlin, New York and Stockholm, Mike and Conny Karlsson Lundgren decided to settle down in Sweden. Mike, the cofounder and creative director of Hall & Lundgren, and Conny, a visual artist working in film and installation, now live in an apartment in the Kungsholmen neighborhood of Stockholm. "When Mike first saw the apartment, he really liked that it was a classic turn-of-the-century home with lots of large windows in a row," Conny says. The previous tenant had lived like a hermit for 40 years and hadn't let anyone inside, so when the landlord began renovations, a simple structure was revealed underneath decades of wallpaper and ornaments. Once stripped back, the apartment was redecorated based on the couple's shared tastes. "There are a lot of things we collected throughout our lives that are now mixed together," Conny says. "Since we both moved around a lot, we've become good at not bringing home stuff that we don't love. Although we have very similar aesthetics, there's still a give-and-take that helps us find a good and realistic balance." For example, the walls are painted industrial shades of gray while the bulk of their furniture is made of warm materials such as vintage wood. Conny and Mike have also amassed many close friends over their years of cross-continental living, which means there are often people visiting them for extended stays. The couple shares the responsibility of cooking for these catch-up dinners, with meals ranging from simple

dishes made with quality ingredients to Conny's specialty: delicious dumplings. "When we first moved back to Sweden, we longed for traditional Swedish fare," he says. "Now I often persuade Mike to try to replicate the great meals we've had on our travels." As much as they enjoy hosting, they also use their home as a place to find respite from their busy schedules: They never bring work into the kitchen or bedroom areas, and they also like to reserve certain spaces for more personal connections. "Since we end up around the big dining table for large gatherings and for work, we like to sit down at the tiny table in the kitchen when it's just the two of us," Conny says. "We always have breakfast together—the first one up makes sure to start the drip coffee! We put our computers and cell phones away so we can have a nice, meaningful conversation with each other." When seeking moments of quiet, they also like to garden on their sunny balcony where they grow mint, sage and tomatoes while watching people play in the park below. They're not the only ones who like the proximity to an open green space: Their puppy, Eddie, often jostles for quality time of her own. "She's quite stubborn and persistently wants to be included," Conny says. "She usually ends up sleeping in one of our laps while we work or are having dinner."

In the following essay on page 336, we suggest ways to divide work and living areas when they occupy the same space in both our homes and heads.

331

Left: Mike and Conny often work at home from their large central dining table. They assembled this light fixture using materials from a hardware store specializing in refurbished original electric parts.

Above Left: Some of their favorite books are *Confessions of a Mask* by Yukio Mishima, the collected works of Marguerite Duras and the collected works of Bruce Weber. The 1960s glass vase on the shelf is a flea-market find.

WORDS : DANIELLE DEMETRIOU

A SEPARATE
SPACE

The art of working from home involves finding the right balance between focusing on the task at hand and knowing when to switch off your computer (and your mind). Here are some ideas for how to divide and conquer your work and play spaces.

Working from home has its benefits, such as avoiding the daily commute, unlimited tea on tap, silence when required, the distance from office politics and the creativity-boosting freedom of a flexible schedule. But the pitfalls can also be plentiful, such as the sudden lure of domestic chores when confronted with unsavory work or the temptation to send emails using one hand while cooking dinner with the other. The art of working from home involves finding a delicate balance between focusing and switching off, ideally in the right place at the right time. Even if you manage to ignore the siren call of the vacuum cleaner while on deadline, this can be trickier than it sounds. Here are a few suggestions for creating a healthy home office.

Create a Work Zone
Modern-day emailing often takes place in the most unlikely domestic settings—lying in bed, sitting at the kitchen table or floating in the bath to name a few. Our ability to work anywhere makes the need for physical boundaries between work and nonwork spaces in the home imperative. The trick is to create a clearly defined work zone that's as self-contained as possible so that when your devices are laid to rest, so is your brain. This might mean clearing out a spare room and turning it into an office or setting up shop in the garage. For those living in smaller spaces, choose a corner of your studio apartment to transform into a dedicated work area.

Put Up Walls
You can create mental boundaries by using physical ones, but that doesn't need to mean bricks and mortar. Using folding antique screens, which can be found at vintage stores or yard sales, you can create a visual frontier between you and your to-do list, or try cocooning your office inside a mini homemade vertical garden by decorating a simple wooden bookcase with dense green plants.

Tidy Your Brain
Clutter is the nemesis of the home-office worker—mountains of documents, technology and stationery threaten to take over precious personal space. One strategy to counter this is to keep things as hidden as possible: This not only keeps your outgoing mail from intruding on the aesthetic sensibilities of your dining room table but is also beneficial because an uncluttered space means an uncluttered brain. Try compartmentalizing your work ephemera into well-labeled confined spaces—this could take the form of stacking towers of old shoeboxes neatly under the desk or using an old chest of drawers as a filing system.

Open the Curtains
The positive impact natural light has on our health and happiness is well documented. Researchers at Chicago's Northwestern University have discovered that offices with generous windows increase their workers' vitality, encourage healthier sleep patterns and improve their overall health and quality of life. With this in mind, try to position your home office where there's plenty of natural light so you can feel the sun's warmth and notice the passing of the seasons.

Spoil Yourself
As with anything in life, working at home should involve a little pleasure. Indulging in a few beautiful work-related objects and taking moments to slow down to enjoy them can do wonders for the busy mind. Handmade stationery or a smooth-flowing fountain pen can add an element of joy to otherwise tedious tasks. Limiting the use of these special products to work hours can also create something to look forward to during your day: To refresh your mind, try preparing aromatic teas using a teapot reserved only for work hours, or listen to playlists saved for office days to help your brain focus and enhance creativity.

Keep Time
To maintain a happy home office, it's important to manage work time clearly and efficiently. Everyone has a personal rhythm: Some work best at 4 a.m. while others prefer conventional daytime office hours. Regardless of your ideal time slot, it's useful to establish a routine so the mind knows when to switch off. Creating a schedule can also help minimize the temptation to procrastinate when suddenly appealing house chores appear, such as dusting the baseboards or color-coding your sock drawer.

HIDEKI

& JUNKO

TAKAYAMA

Hideki and Junko Takayama traded urban living for life in rural Japan to feel more in touch with their senses. Their home in Mashiko, a small town in the Tochigi prefecture 50 miles north of Tokyo, is surrounded by rice-paddy fields and undeveloped woodlands that go on for miles. "There are no other houses near us, which has really helped us slow down, calm our minds and appreciate the changing seasons," says Hideki, a woodworker and furniture maker. The lack of man-made construction intensifies the beauty of the natural landscape, especially on snowy winter nights when the stars shine bright in the absence of artificial lighting. "I love standing by the rice fields in early summer, watching as the reflection of the sunset makes its way across the lake," he says. "In the fall, the ripened rice branches sway in the wind and look like the waves of a golden sea and teach us about the various wind patterns." Living here also gives the couple access to the beautiful plum and cherry trees that are scattered across the nearby mountains: The plum trees start flowering in the spring and the cherry flowers appear just as the plum blossoms begin to fall. Junko loves decorating their house with beautiful ikebana flower arrangements and believes that they're the perfect expression of each season. "We often invite our friends over for a celebratory banquet to watch the plum flowers blossom," Hideki says. Building their house from the ground up was an arduous task—after friends helped lay down the building's foundation, the pair went about

assembling the house bit by bit. "It's been 13 years since we started the building process and, to be honest, it's still a work in progress," Hideki says. While he received a few household items as gifts, Hideki made most of the furniture himself. "The thing I value most when making furniture is the sensation you have when interacting with its textural elements," he says. "I always finish a piece of work by touching it intently and only stop working when it feels perfect." Mashiko is home to many potters who flocked to the area to learn from the late acclaimed Japanese ceramist and former resident Shōji Hamada—the couple's home contains many ceramic home wares, including works by Harvey Young, Akio Nukaga and San Francisco–based company Heath Ceramics. In keeping with the uncluttered, meditative lifestyle they've cultivated in Mashiko, Hideki and Junko don't own a television. Instead, they love gathering for a meal at the end of the day to talk and connect with each other, especially when their teenage son, Genki, is home visiting from abroad. "A house truly becomes a home when you fill it with people's feelings and stories," Hideki says. "Living here means I don't have to be tied down by the values of urban cities, my time is my own and I get to savor the changing of the seasons with the ones I love."

In the following essay on page 348, we consider how a home changes form and meaning throughout the year's seasons.

Previous Page: Hideki and Junko found their antique wood-burning fireplace at a nearby home store. The sofa was a gift from his parents and the bench is one of his own creations.

Above: Hideki designed these wooden bottle sculptures and the table was made using various pieces of old materials.

Following Page: The couple enjoys spending time in the kitchen. This is one of their creations, a daikon salad with rapeseed oil and plum vinegar.

WORDS : MARGARET EVERTON

SEASONAL
ADAPTIONS

Our homes can be adapted to fit the changing seasons in the same way we modify our clothing to suit the daily climate. As we respond to the whims of the weather, we can gain a greater appreciation for just how responsive our dwellings truly are.

The ancient Greek philosopher Heraclitus once said that constancy is an illusion. No matter how modern and stabilized our lifestyles might become, the world around us shifts and changes as it always has—and that includes the seasons. When we pay attention to these continual shifts in nature, we can better understand the effect that the weather has on our homes and our time spent in them.

Summer and winter can be dramatic and indiscreet, requiring domestic vigilance. Our entire space seems to take on an additional hibernating coat during the cooler months—we add layers by putting rugs over bare floors, pile thicker duvets on beds and drape wool blankets over armchairs. Half a year later, sweltering temperatures call for sparseness and openness—we strip down rooms to their bare necessities and fling open the windows to let a breeze flow through, as if the house itself is gasping for a breath of fresh air.

Autumn and spring require subtler adaptations to our home lives. We make provisional movements in these transitional months, gathering and protecting for what's to come, an unfolding and a reawakening. We might stockpile kindling in anticipation of that first icy night or repair screen doors and secure hammocks while waiting for warmer weather. As we continually refine our ability to observe the seasons, we can learn to take cues from the elements, meet the needs of our home and open ourselves up to a more natural way of living.

The seasons can also vastly impact what we do in our homes, not just the way we adorn them. During summertime, our dwellings reflect how the warm weather makes us feel both expansive and languid. We sprawl out over cooler surfaces both inside and out, the boundary between the two seemingly dissolving into one existence. We leave sandals, satchels and sand-crusted novels around the house like shoreline seashells, easy to grab for spontaneous adventures. We tend to dine later and lazier, lingering over lighter meals we prepared while avoiding the stifling oven.

The cold, dark days of winter find us baking more or hovering around open wood fires and clusters of candles, seeking out even the smallest amount of heat and light. We tend to take life back indoors and unapologetically disconnect from the alfresco activities we love during the dog days. But in the winter, we tighten and cushion the perimeters of our domicile to create our own snug cocoon and burrow in this comfort-based atmosphere.

Responding to our home's quarterly changes can make it a highly individualized place to live. We begin to understand the needs and quirks of this living, sentient organism, and we tend to love our homes all the more for each of these oddities: We know the trick for unjamming the swollen side door in the summer, where to step to avoid the creaky floorboards and which living room chair is most exposed to a brisk draft.

Being aware of a home's seasonal shifts takes architecture beyond simple beauty and function—it creates a symbiotic relationship where home and dweller are continually influencing each other. So let's open our doors to the first returning birdsong, flood our bedrooms with midsummer dawns, bake more frosty-day goodies and embrace that we can intimately understand our homes only when we follow the nuances of their movement, forever adapting and evolving.

DITTE ISAGER

& CHRISTIAN

VANG

When photographer Ditte Isager first saw the listing for her home, she recognized a tattered charm that immediately drew her to the structure. "It looked a little like Sleeping Beauty's castle from the outside, but the inside was just a mess," she says. "Nothing had been done since the '70s. You couldn't see the facade as it was covered with ivy and you couldn't even open the windows." Despite the disarray, she and her husband, Christian Vang, were immediately drawn to both its potential and its proximity to Ditte's family, which led them to conducting months of renovations in exchange for their fairy-tale home. "We love the area of Brønshøj and think it's a perfect place to grow," Ditte says. Before they moved in, the home had been passed down through three generations of the same family since its construction in 1913—a connection that Ditte found meaningful. "I grew up in a neighborhood very similar to this 10 minutes from here. I lived in a double house with my grandparents on one floor and us on the other. It was a perfect way to grow up," she says. "I'm really close to my family and feel very lucky to live so close by." With an appreciation for familial bonds and every intention of honoring the home's past, Ditte and Christian set out to remodel and add their own chapter to the home's history while keeping the structure's original features in mind. "We found the original drawings of the house, as it was very important for us to take it back to how it looked when it was

built," Ditte says. "We had to replace everything—roof, windows, bath, kitchen—but we did this so it would look like it did originally." Today she finds pleasure in the way her house contrasts with her former life in New York City, where the couple lived for half a decade before moving back to Copenhagen. "After five years of waking up to a jackhammer, you really appreciate the sounds of birds singing from a tree," she says. Their move back home was also partially influenced by having a son, Wilder: After living in a cramped fifth-floor apartment in New York, they yearned for more space and a slower pace of life. "Having a child changes what you value, but in a good way. And I was so ready for this change," Ditte says. As Ditte and Christian embrace their new life in this old home, they look beyond their family's support system to their neighbors, who gave them a playhouse for Wilder and then arrived with tools to put it together. "They even brought food to celebrate Wilder's 'playhouse housewarming'—it ended up being an amazing summer evening with kids playing in the garden all night, a barbecue and bubbles," Ditte says. "Evenings like that make me think there's nowhere in the world I'd rather be living than right here."

In the following essay on page 358, we explore the ways that homes gain meaning as dwellers leave behind their personal histories.

Above: Some of Ditte and Christian's most treasured pieces of art are a picture of their house that an artist painted in the 1950s, an image by his favorite photographer, Todd Hido, and a still life painted by Christian's father-in-law.

Above Right: The art in the stairwell is by Hugo Guinness.

WORDS : ANNU SUBRAMANIAN

MAKING
HISTORY

A home's former dwellers always leave behind traces of themselves and the lives they lived. By looking closely at the stories they've left in their wake, we're reminded of the history we're making ourselves.

Time capsules act as a greeting to our future selves. Pledging not to revisit its contents for some years, we bury a box full of the items that tell the best story of ourselves: newspaper clippings, family photos, ticket stubs, love letters. They're made up of the details we believe are most emblematic of who we are—a representation of the self we've curated for a moment in time.

Houses that have been standing for generations are no different. In this way, old homes act as multiroom time capsules: They hold lifetimes of memories and snippets from family gatherings, lazy mornings and frenetic afternoons long passed.

We see evidence of the other feet that once wandered the halls of these storied structures, such as a secret space in a dusty corner that may have once been a war bunker or notches marking someone else's height along a wall. We explore the history of the space we live in and learn about the generations of people who sat next to this very window, observing the neighborhood in a different era. We can't help but wonder what led to their decision to knock down a certain wall or paint another deep red. We ponder the unknown: What meals were cooked on these counters? Did young lovers kiss in this entryway? What late-night thoughts crossed the minds of the folks who once slept in this room that gets no light?

While we marvel at the choices of bygone eras that shaped where we stand today, we also contribute our own additions. After observing glimmers of past lives, it's now our turn to bring ourselves into the space and add our own notches, contributing another era's stories to the home's time capsule. While preserving the past, we become part of its future.

Honoring the memories of previous dwellers doesn't mean writing with quills by candlelight, breaking your scrawl only to puff more air on a fireplace's dying embers. Present-day realities may need to supersede the design choices of the past, as what was important half a century ago might not be necessary anymore. But make these changes with thought and care: Like a sculptor crafting a work of art by chipping away at an obelisk, we create a house that suits our needs by making gradual changes to the place so many have called home.

An old home is evocative of the past, rife with stories, stained with imperfections, swirling with imagination. It's the coming together of an unknown past and an unknown future. So as we add our own memories to our spaces, consider that these places are, in many ways, bigger than us. As we share our lives with its future inhabitants, what tales will people imagine based on the clues we leave behind? Life in an old home may be an ongoing act of care and respect for what came before, but it also turns us into a character in someone else's future.

JANIE JACKSON

& CHRISTIAN

PRESTON

Janie Jackson believes the 1860s Victorian house she lives in with her partner, Christian Preston, in London's North Kensington neighborhood reflects the connection between a house's tangible structure and a homeowner's inner world. "A home is more than a backdrop for performing daily tasks and rituals. If its occupants live there with a sense of connectedness, they'll shape the emotional landscape and feeling of that house," she says. Growing up in a picturesque rural area of Southwest England called the Cotswolds, Janie inherited an appreciation for thoughtful practices that create a sense of rootedness and calm. Seeking something organic and familiar when she moved to the city, she used the serene landscape of her childhood as inspiration for her decor in London. "The bareness and rawness of the house helps me feel like I'm in the English countryside," she says. Janie, an interior designer, likes to surround herself with items from her rural past—the kitchenware she inherited from her mother is particularly valuable to her. "The largish cooking pot she used the most is battered and dented, and the mismatching lid was replaced from another of her pots," she says.

These well-loved and well-used tokens are a direct expression of her mother's nurturing nature and serve as a daily reminder for her to keep those traditions alive. The couple believes that a home is made special by the dwellers' active efforts to extend warmth and comfort toward family and guests, such as the way Christian often spends Sunday evenings prepping dinner for Janie and his two teenage children, Caspar and Hebe. Another way they've applied this value to their home is by softening the sharper lines of the mid-century modern furniture with natural embellishments. "I bring back giant hogweed from the Cotswolds at the end of summer, and I also bring in anything cut from the garden, such as the remaining tendrils of the golden hop, and put them by the fireplaces," Janie says. These aren't the only elements they think about when creating a rustic atmosphere in the city: Janie also considers senses that go beyond the tactile and visual. "Smells are important too: I burn sage and oils with woodsy tones of cedarwood, black pepper, eucalyptus, rosemary and cinnamon," she says. "In small but significant ways, I'm trying to gather nature around us."

Above: Janie adores these ceramics by Bridget Tennent—a potter who specializes in hand-thrown porcelain and slip-cast vessels—for their beauty, stillness and austerity. She often moves the pots around to see how they interact with each other and the space in their home.

Above Right: Some of Janie and Christian's favorite linens are Hungarian and French natural hemp cloths and naturally dyed sheets from a maker in Gloucestershire. The couple uses an old traditional Indonesian bedside table and often burns lavender, geranium and patchouli before bed.

WHEN THOU ART KIND

Words by
HELEN DALSTON

Music by
F. J. NETTLEFOLD

A. WEEKES & Cⁱⁱᵉ LTD.

THANK YOU

First, we'd like to thank the people featured in this book for welcoming us into their homes and sharing their stories with us. It has been wonderful to get to know all of you. Thank you for your hospitality and generosity: This book simply wouldn't exist without you.

Thanks to the *Kinfolk* editorial team: Amy Woodroffe, Georgia Frances King, Anja Verdugo, Gail O'Hara, Rachel Eva Lim, Alica Forneret and Kelsey Snell for your creative energy, hard work and dedication—you brought this book to life. We'd also like to thank the team's friends and family for the back rubs, pep talks and coffee deliveries that kept everyone going!

Thanks to Charlotte Heal for leading the design layout of the book and for bringing your keen creative eye to every printed detail.

Thanks to the photographers for beautifully capturing the personalities, decor and stories inside each and every home. It's been an honor and a privilege to work with such a talented group. Thanks also to the fantastic freelance writers and stylists who contributed their visions to the book.

Thanks to our extended community of friends around the world for helping us find and connect with the people featured in this book. Special thanks to Sakiko Setaka, Yukiko Sekine, Sarah Rosenbloom, Elisenda Coll, Lauren Elliot and Margo Lauras. Thanks also to Kota Engaku, Mayumi Yamase and Masafumi Kajitani at *Kinfolk Japan* and Somyung Oh and Sangmin Seo from *Kinfolk Korea*.

Thanks to Tina Minami Dhingra for your production assistance in Japan, for being our local liaison and bridging language barriers. Thank you to Mie Takamatsu for translating the Japanese interviews and profiles and for meeting our crazy deadlines. Special thanks to Kristina Chelberg for providing the final set of eyes on the profile copy.

Thanks to our publisher Lia Ronnen at Artisan for supporting and challenging us throughout the project. Thanks also to Artisan team members Bridget Heiking, Kara Strubel, Nancy Murray, Hanh Le, Sibylle Kazeroid and Allison McGeehon.

Thanks to the creative talents and residents who aren't featured in these pages for their time and energy. Special thanks to Akira and Maya Mada, Bradley Duncan and Samer Fawaz, and Ginés Gorriz and Elina Vila D'Acosta-Calheiros. We'd also like to thank Ditte Isager, Emil Eskesen, Christine Rudolph, Britt Vinther-Jensen and Martha Mulholland.

Special thanks to the people who helped in many ways to bring the images to life, including Amanda Elmore, Julia Hallengren, Tomika Davis, Dominik Panasiuk, Zuza Sowinska-Bania, Takayoshi Tsukisawa, Miriam Robstad, Natalia Mleczak and Cleo at One Management. We'd also like to thank the agents, including Anna Ploman, Rob Magnotta, Willie Mullins and Donna Cerutti. Thanks also to Garbo Interiors and NK Inredning.

And lastly, we want to thank our readers for their continuous support. Without all of you, we wouldn't be able to create the stories we love.

CREDITS

PHOTOGRAPHY

STYLING

WRITING

ILLUSTRATION

Library of Congress Cataloging-in-Publication Data

Williams, Nathan
The Kinfolk Home: Interiors for Slow Living / Nathan Williams.
                  pages cm
ISBN 978-1-57965-665-2
Design and Interiors. 2. Architecture. I. Title.
TX737.W54 2015
641.5'3—dc23

Design by Charlotte Heal

Artisan books are available at special discounts when purchased in bulk for
premiums and sales promotions as well as for fund-raising or educational
use. Special editions or book excerpts also can be created to specification.
For details, contact the special sales director at the address below, or send
an email to specialmarkets@workman.com.

Published by Artisan
A division of Workman Publishing Company, Inc.
225 Varick Street
New York, NY 10014-4381
www.artisanbooks.com

Published simultaneously in Canada by Thomas Allen & Son, Limited

Printed in Singapore
First printing, October 2015

10 9 8 7 6 5 4 3 2 1